Phil Dudman is a gardening presenter on ABC Radio, Channel Nine and Prime TV. He contributes to a number of national magazines and appears regularly at major gardening events across the country.

Phil was the recipient of the Australian Horticultural Media Award for the best gardening radio program or series.

PHIL DUDMAN

the garden guru II

More top tips from Australian gardeners

ABC
Books

Published by ABC Books for the
AUSTRALIAN BROADCASTING CORPORATION
GPO Box 9994 Sydney NSW 2001

Copyright © Phil Dudman 2006

First published August 2006

National Library of Australia
Cataloguing-in-publication entry:
Dudman, Phil.
    The garden guru II: more top tips and hints for gardeners.

    ISBN 10: 0 7333 1942 4
    ISBN 13: 978 0 7333 1942 6

    1. Gardening - Australia. II. Australian Broadcasting
    Corporation. II. Title.

635.0994

Cover and internal design by Christabella Designs
Cover illustrations by Lloyd Foye, Lake Shore Graphics
Typeset in 10.5/14pt Minion by Kirby Jones
Printed and bound by Griffin Press, South Australia

5 4 3 2 1

Acknowledgements

Thank you to all of the backyard garden gurus across Australia who have contributed to this valuable collection of ideas. I can't wait to put them into action in my own garden. I must also express a very big THANK YOU to every one of the ABC celebrity garden gurus who kindly sharing your time and experiences.

There are many people behind the scenes to thank as well: Jane Munro and Richard Johnston, for their kind and dedicated assistance throughout; Andy Henley, for his solid support for this national project; Erica Mann, for producing the marvellous radio promos; Graeme Stuart and Margaret Jovanovich from the ABC North Coast 'Good Gardening' program; and to all of the ABC Radio announcers across the land who have supported our ongoing search for Australia's greatest backyard gardening tips.

I'd especially like to thank my family and my wife, Melissa, for their love and support.

Phil Dudman

Disclaimer

All of the gardening tips published in this book have been collected in good faith. Neither the author nor ABC Books can take any responsibility for the effectiveness of these tips. However, they're all worth a try, so why don't you get out into your garden and give them a go!

Contents

Introduction

It's mind-boggling to think that the deep sense of satisfaction I feel when turning the soil, planting something and watching it grow is the very same simple joy that gardeners would have felt 10 years ago, 50 years ago, even hundreds of years ago. It's good to know that in these ever-changing times, one thing that doesn't change is gardening and the immense pleasure it brings to people all over the world.

Often I think how blessed I am to have discovered this passion for growing things. In my travels I have been fortunate to meet gardeners of all ages from all parts of Australia: so many wonderful down-to-earth people. It is always heartwarming to see the instant friendly rapport that exists between gardeners. One thing that particularly excites me is the marvellous exchange that occurs between gardeners and the sharing of valuable knowledge, based on experience.

For the past few years, I have been on a mission to record some of this wisdom for future generations of gardeners to enjoy.

The first Garden Guru book was packed with practical ideas contributed by dedicated gardeners from every corner of the country. It was well received everywhere, and now gardeners all over the place are benefiting from the precious information that has been passed on. Perhaps the most delightful effect of the first book is the way it has inspired others to share their ideas and experiences.

We realised there was still a lot more wisdom to be documented. In March 2006, via the extraordinary local ABC Radio network, we put out another call to gardeners across the land to send in their tips. In addition, we asked some of Australia's most respected ABC celebrity gardeners to share some of their own experiences.

It's been a great honour to compile this book and a most enjoyable journey. I hope you enjoy these ideas as much as I have.

Phil Dudman

Building and planting your garden

Some people dream of going away for the weekend while a team landscapers comes in and gives their backyard a lightning-fast makeover. Real gardeners prefer to create it themselves. It could take a lifetime to finish — but they don't mind — that's the whole point of having a garden.

But when you're starting from scratch, the whole project can seem pretty daunting. There's nothing like getting a bit of advice from a friendly neighbour who's done it all before.

When we asked around the gardening community, lots of people chimed in with their simple and practical ideas on building a garden.

Site survey

When you're planning a new garden, take plenty of time to observe your property before you dig your first hole. Study the seasons as they change, the length of the shadows that are cast, where the sunny and hot spots are and where it may get boggy. With that information, you can truly plan for a magnificent garden, whether you're planting vegies and fruit trees, natives, exotics or all of the above!

Maree Beveridge, Jilliby, NSW

Do it right

One thing I have learnt from many years of gardening is that it's a waste of time and energy trying to garden in poor soil. On my terrible patch of earth, I have dug in load after load of compost and manure and stayed with the plants that are most suited to our area. The results have been amazing. I have even won a competition or two!

G Hicks, Goonellabah, NSW

Serious soil preparation

I have landscaped many gardens since the 1970s and swear by the following method for preparing garden beds. When you are starting a new garden, hire the services of a bobcat or excavator to dig a 600mm-deep trench below your proposed garden beds. Fill the trenches with rock, rubble or cheap fill before covering them over with the excavated soil, and then top it off with a thick layer of mulch. The mounded soil improves the drainage, and the rock-filled trenches act as water reservoirs that make moisture available to plants when needed.

Alan Caldwell, Woodville, NSW

Tough terrain

Finding it hard to establish new plants on steep hillsides or slopes? Rugged rock swales could be your solution. First, get hold of some heavy galvanised mesh netting and cut it with pliers or snips into pieces about 1m wide and 2m long. Then fold each piece over into a sausage shape and stitch it up with malleable wire using pliers or a large chaff bag needle. Leave one end open, fill the basket with rocks, then stitch it closed. Don't make the bags too heavy, as you want to be able to move them. Around each new plant, lay one of these rock swales in a horseshoe shape with the ends going up-slope. You now have a portable silt and moisture trap. Over time, it creates a stable dam for moisture and nutrient retention, and the soil creatures love them, as do the underlying roots. Tough mulch for where it's tough going! These are resistant to elements, including heavy rain and fire, so they last a long time. Once plantings become established, you can move the swales to protect other parts of the garden. And please resist the temptation to rob rocks from natural areas or your own place. Rocks are an important part of natural habitats! Look to alternatives like crushed concrete or quarry material. Smaller containers filled with sand or soil will do the trick, too. You are limited only by your imagination!

Harry Kruze, Wurtulla, Qld

Find a mentor

When we started gardening many years ago, we were 'mentored' by a fine English gentleman named Harry Coops. He was a botanist who'd led early tours of the WA wildflowers for the WA railways. One of his most memorable quotes was, 'The more plants you have in the garden, the less weeds you have.' If there's an empty spot, put a plant in it. He also advised that whenever you plant, toss a couple of leaves of the plant into the bottom of the hole. It helps to activate all the good bacteria in the soil.

Margaret Graham, Stoneville, WA

Handy pond liner

A lot of in-ground ponds incorporate a flexible butyl rubber pond liner. Usually, it sits on a layer of sand which provides a buffer between the soil and the liner. We have found that newspaper also makes a good buffer, and it's far easier to work with because it holds its position better than sand. Simply line the pond area with newspaper (6 sheets is a good thickness) then put down the liner.

Warren Sheather, Yarrowyck, NSW

Amphibian ladders

Ponds provide frog-friendly environments in the garden, but often the steep and slippery sides of ponds are difficult for young frogs to climb. We plant heavily textured ground covers (particularly *Myoporum parvifolium*) around the perimeter of our ponds. They create little 'amphibian ladders', so the young frogs can enter and exit the water with ease, and they also soften the edges of ponds visually.

Warren Sheather, Yarrowyck, NSW

Totally hooked

Fishing line is an effective low-cost support for climbing plants and it's easy to replace if you have to cut it down to paint a wall or prune the plant. Just thread it across some kind of guide. On a timber fence, I use fence staples about 1m apart; and on brick walls, I find concrete screws very useful.

Christine Chapman, Burringbar, NSW

Building a garden community

Over the years, I have run numerous 'plant swap' days at my place. Local gardeners bring along 'tough' plant cuttings; enjoy a cuppa, a nibble and a chat; collect other gardeners' cuttings; cut and dig in my garden; and go home happy in the knowledge that they are expanding their garden at no cost. It's always a terrific day. Using only these 'tough' plants, I have extended my garden from ½ha (1 acre) to 5 times that size!

Patricia Gabb, Beaufort, Vic

Plant clusters

One of the best things you can do when building a new garden is to group together plants of similar needs. This makes the job of feeding, watering and pruning your garden much easier and more efficient.

Malcolm McKinlay, Singleton, NSW

Value plants

If you have a small garden, choose your plants carefully. Look for the ones that have more than one feature, such as shape, form, flowers, perfume, colour and produce. Try to get maximum value for your planting space.

Nola McRae, Wagga Wagga, NSW

High risers

In all my years living in a high-rise apartment, I have wasted far too much money on failed planting attempts. Finally I have found a group of attractive plants that more than meet the challenges, bromeliads. They have adorable foliage and flowers; they are tough and wind-tolerant; they prefer to grow in light potting mediums, which is good; they never get too big, so don't need pruning; and they grow lots of pups which are easy to separate and propagate. What am I going to spend my money on now?

Vicki Cashin, Bronte, NSW

Paint it white

A flowerbed devoted to pure white blooms always looks fresh, crisp and elegant. An added bonus; the blooms shine in the night like little lights while other flower colours go unnoticed.

Nola McRae, Wagga Wagga, NSW

Shady spots

The attractive green-and-white foliage of hostas makes a gorgeous addition to a moist cool shady spot, especially under large deciduous trees. Give them a backdrop of lacy ferns and watch their large leaves light up!

Nola McRae, Wagga Wagga, NSW

The art of observation

Take a good look through the garden every day. Look out for pest outbreaks, and note growth and flowering periods and the like. Look up any new insects you discover to see if they are friend or foe. Jot down these observations as diary notes in a garden journal. It makes a terrific tool for seasonal planning and maintaining your own garden.

Barbara Benham, Stanthorpe, Qld

Don't overdo it

If you are going to transplant something heavy, such as a large tree from a pot into the garden, don't do it by yourself. Make sure you get someone to give you some help. I tried to do it alone and hurt my back. Sadly, it put me out of gardening action for a whole month!

Eunice Curran, Griffith, NSW

The world is your garden

Running out of space to plant? Don't stop at your fence line. With the blessing of our local council, we have transformed the next-door drainage area from a neglected rubbish dump of weeds into an inviting gully that's alive with exotics, flowering natives, citrus and other fruit trees. Our efforts have encouraged our downhill neighbours to take up gardening, too. Now they take responsibility for the common areas we share by planting, weeding, mulching and composting. It's been wonderful for building our community.

Lolli Forden, Smithfield, Qld

Gloves for every occasion

Having particular gloves for particular garden tasks makes you a lot more comfortable and ready for action. Leather rigger gloves are good for heavy-duty pruning. Use suede gardening gloves for rough weeding work; they are soft, pliable and tough. Thin disposable gloves are best for fiddly hand-weeding, planting out seedlings, and squishing pests.

Barbara Benham, Stanthorpe, Qld

Keeping nails clean

Even wearing gardening gloves won't stop your fingernails from becoming ingrained with dirt. Before you go into the garden, scratch your nails through a cake of soap. This prevents a build-up of soil and washes out easily with the aid of a nail brush.

Jan Johnson, Emerald, Vic

Gardener's hand-cleaner

Mix together 1 part lemon juice, 1 part glycerine and 1 part rosewater. Rub over your hands to keep them smooth and clean.

A Drummond, Capalaba, Qld

Care for the hands that create

If you're like me and you prefer to garden without gloves, liberally apply gardener's wax (a really heavy barrier cream) before going out to play in your little piece of Eden. When washing your hands after gardening, add lavender-scented disinfectant, lavender oil or tea-tree oil to the hot water and scrub heartily. Then dry your hands well before moisturising them. It won't save you from every splinter but it will protect you against many nasties as well as leaving your hands feeling fresh and smelling divine.

Elaine Harris, Burnie, Tas

Compost, worms and mulches

Build a healthy soil in your garden and your plants will thrive. It seems a simple formula but it's half the secret to successful gardening. Regularly apply organic matter, such as compost, worm castings and mulches. They nourish the soil — and all the beneficial organisms that live in it — and provide plants with nature's own slow-release fertiliser. They also help to retain valuable moisture, which means we use less water in our gardens.

It doesn't take much to convince Aussie gardeners of the benefits. In fact, most of them are totally obsessed with the stuff!

Secret recipe

The magic of compost has helped transform our barren quarry of shale and clay into a delightful garden filled with wonderful and healthy plants. I liken composting to good cooking: a variety of local ingredients in small doses, spiced with manures, potash and blood and bone. I view this recycling as a way of caressing the earth. My compost bin overflows, and I'm always experimenting and making my own compost tea elixir.

Lolli Forden, Smithfield, Qld

Now for the good news

I shred all spare paper that comes into my house and use it as mulch or add it to the compost. No paper is wasted. Over time it breaks down and I dig it into the ground when replanting. We don't have a recycling service, so it saves a lot of rubbish going into the bin. It's also very effective and costs nothing.

Chrissy Willis, Kyogle, NSW

Just shred it

The quickest and easiest way to prepare paper for composting or worm farming is with a paper shredder. They don't cost much, and since I have been using shredded paper, the worms have multiplied at an impressive rate. It's a fantastic way to get rid of those unwanted documents lying around. Be sure to soak it in water before you give it to the worms.

Judy Roberson, Tura Beach, NSW

Homemade compost tumbler

You can make a good tumbling compost bin from any cylindrical container that has a lid. You just need to put a steel rod through the centre of the barrel. I have used an old A-frame clothes drying rack to mount the barrel so that it can be spun easily, but I'm sure it would be easy to make up a simple frame with common old tomato stakes. We also use our mulcher mower to prepare any paper or cardboard for composting. First we wet it, then mow over it to chop it up. This gives it a good head start in the composting process.

Julie Dart, Byawatha, Vic

Clean composting

I like to reduce the risk of unwanted disease being introduced to my garden from store-bought produce. I boil up all my fruit and vegie scraps in a large cooking pot and allow them to cool before I add to my compost. This kills all the nasties and it helps the materials to break down much quicker, too.

Norman Ross, Peak Hill, NSW

Can you dig it?

A great way to dispose of all your garden rubbish is to bury it. Once it's done, the site is already dug over, so you can plant it up straightaway. The plant roots will take advantage of the wonderful organic matter in the soil as it breaks down.

Michael Yonwin, Thorneside, Qld

Terra Preta in your backyard

In certain areas of the Amazon Basin, there exists a remarkably fertile soil. Known as Terra Preta, this rich black earth is found where 2000 years ago the indigenous people used to burn to clear their fields before planting. Many experts believe the fertility of this soil comes from the large amounts of charcoal it contains. Charcoal is well known for its ability to absorb other chemicals so it can trap and store plant nutrients that would otherwise be leached from the soil by irrigation and heavy rain. My suggestion is to add crushed charcoal either directly to your soil or preferably to the compost heap in combination with your fertiliser and see if you notice the difference in productivity.

John Hingston, Warrnambool, Vic

Worm farm in a jiffy

Worms do an excellent job of processing household waste and make some of the very best fertiliser available. Yet only 7 percent of Australian households have their own worm farm. Come on! Worm farms are fun and easy to make.

Two polystyrene boxes from the fruit shop will make a cheap and practical worm farm. Broccoli boxes work best. The top box should have drainage holes in the base, while the bottom box should be without holes. Choose a shady spot in your garden. Into the top box place a mixture of 50 percent old cow manure, 30 percent leaf litter or dry grass clippings and 20 percent compost, then wet it and add some composting worms — you can pick them up at your garden centre. When they've wriggled down out of the light, cover the lot with a moistened hessian bag or sheets of newspaper. To prepare their food, put all your kitchen scraps through the food processor. Feed more scraps as needed.

John O'Reilly, Banora Point, NSW

Handy worm bedding

A wonderful bedding material for starting up home worm farms is cat litter made from recycled paper. The worms absolutely love the stuff! Just pour in the pelletised product, add water and watch how quickly the worms enter the substrate, start eating and — very importantly — start breeding! It's an inexpensive, easy-to-use, chemical-free and environmentally sound product.

Bill Hall, Page, NSW

Home worm farm — think big!

Commercially available plastic worm farms tend to be small and poorly insulated against extremes of temperature. Why not build a bigger one out of recycled materials so all garden wastes can be converted into worm castings! Dismantle a couple of old wooden pine pallets then construct a box with the boards. Line the inside with black plastic. Remember, you'll need to include a drainage hole to release — and collect — excess moisture. Add a wooden lid. Leaving a gap on top, put on a tin roof to keep rain off. Lay some bricks or timber on the ground and ensure the box stays about 70mm above this floor. Feed the worms with all your garden wastes — the leafier the better — but include stems and roots, vegetable scraps, and weeds before they seed. To keep everything moist, water every second day.

James Cherry, Nemingha, NSW

Using worm wee

You may ask, what is so good about this wormy wee tea? The earthworms have digested the plant parts, which contain all the nutrients and minerals from the soil in your garden. On top of that, they add some beneficial bacteria to the mix. When you put it in the soil, it fills it with life and helps to unlock the natural goodness.

Worm wee from your homemade worm farm can be applied directly to your soil or diluted and sprayed on the foliage. To make compost tea, every fortnight, harvest some worm castings and mix it in a big drum full of water. Use it on anything you want to thrive. The best time to spread this brew is late afternoon. That gives the plant time to absorb the nutrients overnight while it is cool. If there is a chance of the compost tea burning the leaves in the hot sun the next day, then sprinkle water on the plants in the morning.

Before long you will see and enjoy great results from your own compost tea in your garden. It gives plants a boost and produces very tasty produce.

James Cherry, Nemingha, NSW

Free mulch on hand

At my place, retaining moisture on sloping sandy land is always a challenge. To help overcome this, I mulch continually. I use prunings from my shrubs and strip the leaves from tree branches and spread them around the root zone of the plants below. This is easy and it works. Occasionally, I fork the decomposed mulch into the soil, which helps to improve its sandy texture.

Ailsa Geary, Bateau Bay, NSW

Weed processor

Whenever I'm out pulling weeds, I toss them into a black garbage bag that I drag around with me. When the bag's full, I tie the top and store it out of sight under a bush. It acts as temporary mulch, and in a short time, the internal heat cooks and kills any weed seeds. The remainder of the contents turns into a lovely mulch, ready to use around my plants.

Joyce Neal, Ulverstone, Tas

`Life' in the gutter

I have 'gutter mulch' delivered free from a gutter cleaning company. It's wonderful dark black mulch, and my garden thrives on the stuff. Remember, it's FREE and saves the gutter people taking it to the dump.

Chris Sherlock, Glandore, SA

Grow your own mulch

If you want to rest a bed in your veggie patch or if you have a bit of spare space, why not sow a crop of lucerne? It's easy to grow, but best of all, it's deep-rooted so it draws in many minerals and nutrients way down in the soil. Of course, when you harvest it, it makes an A-grade mulch that breaks down quickly to feed and enrich your soil.

Don Mackay, Margaret River, WA

Top it up

Twice a year, I have 20 bails of pea straw delivered to my place. It's just enough to mulch our entire suburban-sized garden. Over the years, this regular practice has resulted in spectacular growth and marvellous weed suppression. Try it for yourself!

Meredith McQueen, Sandy Bay, Tas

Read all about it

Many gardeners lay newspaper down on the ground before covering it with mulch. It's a simple way to smother and combat weeds while conserving soil moisture. I like to soak the newspapers in liquid fertiliser first. This adds a little extra nutrient to the soil and helps to reduce any nitrogen loss as the newspaper and mulch break down.

GC Loughborough, Beaconsfield, Tas

Garden built on the sheep's back

Shearing and crutching dags make terrific mulch. Why not use wool? It's a great insulator, will smother out weeds like any mulch, holds water and slowly releases any urine into the soil. Perhaps it's the answer to low wool prices!

Reg Kidd, Orange, NSW

More woolly supporters

I use belly and skirting wool that I get from a local farmer, lay it on the ground around my plants then top with compost or some other mulch. The wool keeps the roots cool and helps retain moisture plus it will bed down around your tree, just like a blanket! I find this excellent for trees in a dry spot!

Suzanne Hoffman, Tamworth, NSW

Easy returns

Living in country where it's as dry as dry can be, we never toss out anything if we can possibly recycle it in the garden. We have old carpet from the house in the veggie patch. This acts like mulch, inhibiting weeds, keeping the plant roots cool and holding in valuable moisture. We don't have a compost bin, but we dig in all scraps and newspapers in the veggie patch. To our surprise, we get more veggies than we plant — from our scraps we get potatoes, pumpkins, beans and tomatoes. With little effort, we even get mushrooms growing from the mushroom compost we use.

Maria-Anna Barry, Leyburn, Qld

(Worm) food for thought

Everyone is a gardener, whether they know it or not. It is only a matter of time before we get involved by becoming compost!

Reg Kidd, Orange, NSW

Feeding your plants

Australian soils are world-renowned — not for their quality but for their lack of nutrients. Feeding plants is a good gardening practice. But for many Australian gardeners, it's an absolute necessary if our gardens are to thrive.

Not surprisingly, we Aussie gardeners have become masters in providing hungry plants with the nourishment they need. This isn't always as straightforward as tossing about a bag of commercial fertiliser. Methods may involve mixing up special brews in the backyard and experimenting with things that most of us have in the kitchen cupboard. The results of this resourcefulness are often staggering.

Why don't you try some of them yourself?

Sweet success

Mix 2 tablespoons unprocessed honey in a 9-litre watering can and pour it all over the root zone of your plants. It's a great little tonic for improving the quality of fruit and vegetables.
Don Mackay, Margaret River, WA

Tea tonic

Soak your used teabags in water for a few days then use this brew to water your ferns. They love it!

Beryl Taylor, Cummins, SA

Mine's bigger than yours

You can proudly say, 'My pumpkin's bigger than yours!' if you feed your vines with a special homemade fertiliser — diluted human urine. You just have to put the thought of the fertiliser to the back of your mind as you sit proudly at the dinner table.

Beverley Morgan, Shepparton, Vic

Caffeine-free canines

Blood and bone is an excellent all-purpose fertiliser for the whole garden. The only problem is, dogs thing they've got a whiff of Nirvana and it sends them into a digging frenzy. To make blood and bone unpalatable to dogs, mix in a small amount of coffee grounds. They can't stand it!

Mark Wall, Lismore, NSW

It's cool

If you're going away for a long weekend, make up some slow-release liquid fertiliser. Mix in a container then pour it into ice-cube trays and freeze. Tip the cubes into your plant pots shortly before you leave home. They will be watered and fed slowly over the weekend and will be looking better than you expected when you return.

Andrew Westwood, Launceston, Tas

Fruit booster

Overripe bananas and banana skins are an excellent fertiliser for my sandy soil. Get your local greengrocer to save you the bananas that would otherwise be thrown out. Dig a hole in the garden, drop a few in the bottom of the hole, partly backfill with soil and plant something over the top. The plants love it!

Ailsa Geary, Bateau Bay, NSW

Googy advice

When you hard-boil eggs, don't throw away the water. Let it cool down and then use it to water your potted plants. The eggshells contain many minerals needed by the plants, and this solution gives pot plants a quick boost.

Julie Buxton, East Victoria Park, WA

Tea weed solution

Soak your used teabags in a jar of diluted seaweed extract. When you are potting plants or planting out seedlings, drop a soaked teabag under the roots for a super-charged start.

Beryl Taylor, Cummins, SA

Magnesium sulphate

Sprinkle Epsom salts around citrus and passion fruit and water it in well. It provides the plants with magnesium and sulphur, which really gives them a burst of vigour.
Joan Miller, Lismore, NSW

The lowdown on Epsom salts

You hear a lot people recommending Epsom salts for this and that. And for good reason. It's a fast-acting source of magnesium and sulphur and helps along many plants, especially if soils are depleted. Here are some suggestions:

1. Fill a 9-litre watering can with water then add 1 level dessertspoon Epsom salts.
2. Water over citrus, gardenias and daphne bushes. It is fine to spray the solution on the leaves. If they are yellowing, the leaves will quickly green up again.
3. It boosts flower growth of daylilies, camellias and azaleas.
4. Helps to blue hydrangeas and improves colour on many other flowers.
5. Improves the development of fruit in tomatoes and capsicum.
6. Sprinkle 1–2 teaspoons around the base of rose bushes — they love it!
7. Sprinkle around maidenhair ferns for strong growth.

Noeleen Ridgway, Ringwood North, Vic

Helen's tonic

This little tonic is excellent for all plants, including natives and acid-loving plants. Apply 4 times a year.

- 1 teaspoon iron chelates
- 1 teaspoon Epsom salts
- 1 teaspoon seaweed extract
- 7 litres water

Mix well and apply it to foliage and root systems.

Helen Whalen, Newcastle, NSW

Thanks, Skip

For an organic fertiliser, I use kangaroo poo. It doesn't smell; it doesn't attract flies; dogs don't want to eat it; and it doesn't burn plants, even when they're young seedlings. It's also suitable for feeding native plants. Collecting it is a lot of fun and teaches you where your friendly 'roo population likes to hang out — that's the spot with lots of pellets! Rather than eat poor old Skippy, we might be better off harvesting her manure. Your plants will be hopping out of the ground!

Muriel Scholz, Laura, SA

Nutrient exchange program

Swap your lawn clippings with your local alpaca farmer in return for droppings. It's an excellent fertiliser that's easy to handle.

Lyndal Money, Boulder, WA

Timely top-up

I have learnt that it works best to feed plants after the warm weather is over and the summer showers have finished (if you get any summer showers). The feed is most needed at this time because rain leaches many nutrients deep into the soil, and the plants need a 'top-up'. This should result in a more productive growing season and healthier plants.

Karen Judith Bittner, Olinda, Vic

Test it first

Don't make the mistake of putting lime on your garden until you have checked the pH reading. If you overdo it, it can make your pH far too alkaline. That's when valuable nutrients start getting locked, and your plants suffer. A simple pH is tester is inexpensive and can be purchased in all good garden centres.

Pat Fitt, Collie, WA

Water-wise tips

With water restrictions a part of life, dedicated and determined gardeners have made many important and changes to the way they use water. Long gone are the days of wild directionless sprinklers spraying valuable moisture up into the atmosphere. Gardeners all over Australia are gardening smarter: adopting good water-saving habits, like mulching to lock in soil moisture, and choosing plants for their drought-hardiness as well as beauty.

Some clever gardeners have taken it further by devising new and creative ways of providing moisture for their plants without waste. Here are some super ideas for you to try yourself.

Local knowledge

Contact your local council to see if they have lists of drought-hardy plant species that are suitable for your area. Often they will also have a free publication that outlines some easy-to-follow water-wise gardening tips.

Reg Kidd, Orange, NSW

Water news

When planting, I always line the hole with several sheets of newspaper (not the colour supplements). Then I fill the hole with water, allow it to drain and plant and backfill with soil that has been improved with old manure. The whole thing receives a good soaking before I apply a thick layer of mulch. The newspaper holds moisture around the roots while the plant is young and getting established. It saves a lot of water, and I have had 100 percent success using this planting method over my 30 years of gardening.

Elizabeth Bradfield, Rosebank, NSW

Mulch it, mulch it

Where I live, we have been in drought for over 10 years, but I still have a 5-acre garden that flourishes. I only plant the toughest of plants, and whenever we get the odd bit of spring rain, I follow up religiously by covering the damp soil with wet newspaper and a good layer of mulch. It really holds the water in, and I only have to water once or twice over the summer.

Patricia Gabb, Beaufort, Vic

Wetting agents work

Each year in late October I toss a granular wetting agent on all garden beds, lawn and potted plants. This helps cut down on water usage because even the lightest shower of rain soaks into the soil instead of running off. Economical 10-litre bags are available at large hardware stores, and about one of two bags of these will do the whole lot.

Noeleen Ridgway, Ringwood North, Vic

Food for thought

The stuff they put in those little pads you find in the base of meat trays is highly absorbent. I use it to help retain moisture in my garden. I soak them, remove the packaging, dilute the contents in water and then pour it over the garden. It's good recycling. I have also used disposable nappies!

Jacky Matthews, Scarborough, Qld

Simple water-saving

I always keep a small watering can on the kitchen sink to collect the cold water while waiting for the hot water to come through. That's what I use on my pot plants inside and out.

Noeleen Ridgway, Ringwood North, Vic

Rain recycler

If you have a down-pipe that leads nowhere, put a big plastic drum or container under it to catch rainwater. After a downpour, lift it out, add seaweed fertiliser and fish emulsion and use it to fertilise your precious plants.

Denise Margaret Lucas, Carindale, Qld

Reverse psychology

When your garden is thirsty and dry
And you look up in vain at the sky
Use bindii spray
And that very same day
The rain will pour down from on high

Judi Cox, Springfield, Qld

Deep watering saves water

Wetting the top surface of the soil is a big waste of water. When watering those special plants (roses, fruit trees etc), push the nozzle of your hose deep into the ground around the roots and give them a really deep soaking for a couple of minutes. You don't have to water as often this way, and your plants will stand up and say, 'Thank you!'

Cecile Carter, Dee Why, NSW

Good option

On dry shaly soils, a weeper hose (the type made from recycled rubber) is extremely effective in establishing young trees and shrubs. Run it for a couple of hours on very low pressure once or twice a month. I have found it far more effective and efficient than drip irrigation or hand watering.

Leigh Murray, Queanbeyan, NSW

Simple water recycling

When you're watering or fertilising hanging baskets, don't let it drain all over the place. Put a bucket underneath to collect the water, then use it somewhere else.

Mary Jones, Wamuran, Qld

Water-well

We have grown vegetables in self-watering (or water-well) type pots with excellent results. There is no wastage with water draining on the pavers or evaporating from an open garden bed. We use a top-quality potting mix and always incorporate additional water-saving granules in the medium to absorb moisture efficiently.

Sharon Greenaway, Strathfieldsaye, Vic

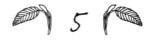

Propagating your own plants

Want to save money in the garden? Then have a go at propagating your own plants. Gardeners have been sharing plants for aeons via seed-saving and passing on cuttings over the fence. It's still the most economical way to increase your stock of plants.

It's also the most satisfying because you know you've done it yourself. It can be a bit tricky at times, but we keep learning from every experience.

Thankfully, many gardeners have come forth and shared the finer details of the techniques they have learnt.

Timing for seed-sowing success

Many seeds have a preferred season in which to be sown. If someone has given you some seed, but you're not sure when you should sow them, try this general rule as a guide. Plants that flower and produce seed from late winter to early summer are best sown in autumn. Those that flower and seed from late summer to early winter are best sown in spring. All you need to do is research when they flower.

Mazza Verdante, Grafton, NSW

Delicate roots

When planting seeds or cuttings in a pot, first line the inside of the pot with newspaper. That way, when you're ready to plant them in the ground, the whole lot comes out easily and intact, so you don't disturb the root system.

Carol Fiorini, Mt Helena, WA

Handy seed template

Place a piece of chicken wire over the top of a seed-raising tray when planting large seeds. It makes an excellent template that ensures even planting.

Brenda Allen, Invermay, Tas

Seed-sowing success

This is my sure-fire way to achieve a good germination rate when sowing seeds. After tilling and preparing your soil, make drills and fill them with a mix of 50 percent river sand and 50 percent soil. Sow your seeds and sprinkle a small amount of river sand over the top. Water in then cover with damp newspaper. As long as you keep the newspaper damp, this will stop the seeds from drying out. As the seeds begin to shoot, remove the newspaper gradually over a few days to sun-harden them.

Peg & Jean Connolly, Uki, NSW

Make your own seed tapes

In a saucepan, dissolve 1 tablespoon cornflour in 1 cup cold water. Cook over a medium heat, stirring constantly to prevent the mixture from getting lumpy. Once it begins to boil and the mixture becomes translucent and gel-like in consistency, remove from the heat and put aside to cool. Tear off a length of paper towelling about 1? metres long. Then cut it lengthwise into 1cm-wide strips. Put a few spoonfuls of the cornflour mixture into a plastic bag. Work the gel towards one corner and snip a small section off the corner. If you are preparing to plant small seeds, make the cut extra small. Next dab the gel along the length of your tape at the correct spacing for your chosen seeds and place a seed onto each dab. For tiny seeds, it may be easier to mix them in with the gel. Label the tape with the name of the seed, allow the gel to dry and then plant the entire tape in the garden.

A Drummond, Capalaba, Qld

Tomato seed

When you find a truly good tasty tomato, slice one thinly and place on paper towels. Date and name the variety and leave it to dry thoroughly. When the time comes for planting in spring, simply lay the paper on some good seed-raising mix, sprinkle some mix on top and water well. The seeds come up in no time. It's a simple method for saving and storing tomato seed.

Beryl Joy, Australind, WA

Growing geraniums from seed

I like to harvest geranium seed when it's quite fresh. Keep an eye on the spent flowers, and when they begin to turn brown, collect the seed early one morning. You will usually find 2–3 packed in a swollen tube at the base of where the flower was. When you remove the outer lining of the tube, small white feathers unfurl, each with a seed attached to the base. Plant them in a good quality seedling mix or into some worm castings, leaving the white feather-like head above the soil. Green shoots should appear within 7–10 days. Transplant the seedlings into tubes as soon as they are large enough to handle.

Mary O'Reilly, Banora Point, NSW

Growing hippeastrums by seed

Growing hippeastrums from seed is easy to do and a terrific way to increase your supply. But you need to follow a few rules. Collect the seed as soon as the seed pods dry and burst open. Plan to sow the seeds straight away because they tend to loose their viability if stored for any more than 3 months. Always use a sterilised seed-raising mix and sow the seed in trays by simply sprinkling the seed over the mix. Cover seed with 3mm of mix and keep it moist but not wet. Shoots will appear within 3 weeks and will grow steadily if fed a little soluble fertiliser every few weeks. In 6 months, your seedling bulbs can be transplanted into the garden and will produce their first flowers after 2 to 3 years.

Annette Zambelli, Modanville, NSW

Growing hippeastrums by cuttage

A great way to propagate, or clone, your favourite hippeastrum bulb is by a successful technique called 'cuttage'. Take a single bulb and cut it vertically into 2, 4 or 8 pieces. Dust the pieces with a fungicide and plant them between layers of sterilised, dampened sphagnum moss. In 4 to 6 weeks, each of the little pieces will begin to sprout. Bulblets with healthy roots and leaves will form about 6 weeks later. The bulblets can then be planted into pots in a free mixture of course sand and peat moss. The best time to carry out this process is from January to March.

Annette Zambelli, Modanville, NSW

Cutting box

Several years ago, I bought a large plastic storage box (50x30x20cm deep) from my local op-shop, drilled holes in the bottom and filled it with coarse river sand. I strike all my cuttings in this and have very few failures.

Noeleen Ridgway, Ringwood North, Vic

No tangles

Place a 10cm pot inside a 14cm pot and fill the gap between the two with propagating mix. Use this arrangement for striking cuttings. You can plant several in the one pot, and there is minimal tangling of roots when you are ready to separate them and pot them on.

Jan Johnson, Emerald, Vic

Stop the rot

If you want to strike cuttings of geraniums, pelargoniums or succulents, it's a good idea to leave them in the shade to dry out for a week or so. The ends callus over so that they don't rot, and they'll strike quite readily.

Penny Pipkorn, Riverside, Vic

It's that easy

One summer, I pruned my gardenias and put the cuttings into a jar of water. I intended to prepare them in a good cutting mix, but forgot all about them. A few weeks later I was delighted to find they had developed roots in the jar of water. I didn't realise they would strike so easily.

Daphne Beaumont, Lismore, NSW

Banksia cuttings made easy

I have always had trouble propagating banksias. By mistake, I left one sitting in a glass of water for a month. When I realised it was still there, I found it shooting madly, whereas others that I put straight into a pot of striking mix had died almost straight away! I planted my lucky success into some potting mix, and off it went. My initial memory lapse has now resulted in 2 very happy banksia bushes.

Meredith Tavener, Medowie, Vic

 6

Pest and disease control

Pest and diseases require prompt action. But it doesn't mean you have to rush down to the local garden centre to pick up a spray. In many cases, you only need to look as far as the kitchen cupboard.

Gardeners all over Australia have been experimenting for years with home remedies and other safe methods of dealing with common pests and diseases. Some of them have been passed down through the generations and made it into this chapter.

Try out these concoctions for yourself.

SNAILS AND SLUGS

Slug domes

This is my sure-fire way of collecting slugs in my fernery. Halve a large grapefruit and remove the fleshy pulp. Make a small opening for the slugs to enter and then place it upside down on the ground to create a dome. Slugs find this a most attractive and tasty place to congregate for dinner and so they leave your plants alone. It also makes it easy to gather up the slugs and dispose of them.

Janet Cielo, Merbein, Vic

Simple snail trap

I have a lot of sandstone rocks bordering my garden. Snails like to congregate behind them for shelter. This makes it easy to collect them in the morning. I feed the snails to my neighbour's chooks in return for eggs. It's a fantastic system.

Thelma Dennis, Bundanoon, NSW

Condy's crystals

A sprinkle of Condy's crystals (potassium permanganate) around precious plants will keep away slugs and snails. It should be replaced after heavy rain as this will dissolve it.

Noeleen Ridgway, Ringwood North, Vic

Battered snails and slugs

I have found plain old plain flour an excellent deterrent for snails. Simply spread it around your seedlings; sprinkle some over the top, too. Slimy bodies seem to find the resulting batter a tad too unpleasant.

KJ Reynolds, Evandale, Tas

Taste this

When I plant seedlings of veggies, I lay cuttings of curry plant, lavender and lemon verbena among them. It's very effective in keeping away snails and slugs.

Melva Bartram, Albany, Vic

Night hunt

My mum used to collect snails 60 years ago only she used a torch at night to nab them.

Thelma Dennis, Bundanoon, NSW

Snail genocide

I have managed to eradicate whole generations of snails from my garden by going around on spring mornings with a bucket of heavily salted warm water, picking them off the underside of leaves and dropping them in.

Noeleen Ridgway, Ringwood North, Vic

Waiting for the crunch

Darkness comes as sunlight dies
And you find with no surprise,
Night in gardens never fails
To attract a million snails.
They slime their way along the grass,

Nibbling on the plants they pass,
Heading for the tasty treat
Of newly planted silver beet
Or tiny shoots of new sprung peas.
No plant more sweet to snails than these.
But hark! I hear a mighty tread
Stamp towards the vegie bed.
And the snails they shake with fear
As the awesome feet draw near.
Who is it comes this Nemesis?
Whose fearsome mighty tread is this?
Whose the boots to be re-soled
With new-crunched bodies green and cold?
Whose approach turns bugs all pale?
A man who loves to stomp a snail!
So if you have a snail plague, too,
Then this has shown you what to do.
When snails begin their nightly munch,
You should do the midnight crunch.

Helen Brumby, Rose Bay, Tas

GRUBS, BUGS AND GRASSHOPPERS

A ticklish tale

Now the grasshoppers munch up your plants
Not your weeds, but the nice ones that aren't.
When the day is still new,
Flush them all down the loo
And hope they don't tickle your aunt.

Judi Cox, Springfield, Qld

Jiminy crickets!

Troublesome grasshoppers can be easy to catch in the mornings and late afternoons, but if you try to nab them at any other time, they move away much too quickly. A good way to trap them at this time is to hypnotise them ... yes, hypnotise them. Look at one straight in the eye and start making a wide circular motion in front of it with your finger. In a spiral fashion, gradually make the motion smaller and closer to the pest. It will stand there in a daze, totally motionless. That's when you grab it! 'Look into my eyes.'

Terry Brampton, Nundah, Qld

Zap zap

The larvae of codling moth make a mess of apples. In springtime, when the codling moths are out ready to lay their eggs in the apple blossoms, I hang a bug zapper in my orchard at dusk. It's a fabulous way to reduce the numbers of theses pests organically, and I've found it has helped to decrease the population of moths over the years.

Julie Dart, Byawatha, Vic

White cedar moth

Hairy caterpillars of the white cedar moth ravage my white cedar tree every year. At night, they climb the trunk to reach the canopy, where they feed on the leaves until the tree is completely defoliated. I have come up with a solution. As soon as the grubs appear, I place two or three bands of 50mm masking tap around the trunk, sticky side out. I check the tree early morning and early afternoon. If there are grubs already in the tree, they will descend in the morning and meet the sticky barrier. In the early evening, caterpillars working their way up will also meet the barrier. Using a brush, I simply dust them off into a bucket of warm soapy water. After a few days, I have collected all of the caterpillars that are about, and my tree keeps its foliage. Also it breaks the life cycle and reduces the number of caterpillars appearing the following season. Don't handle the hairy caterpillars with bare skin because they can cause an irritation.

Sr Pat Bundock OP, Wallangarra, Qld

Woolly insect traps

Wrap some sheep wool around the base of plants and trees to trap damaging bugs and grubs that climb up the stems. If you have any chooks free-ranging about, they will quickly learn where to find the trapped insects, thereby keeping the wool clean.

Lee Fontanini, Manjimup, WA

Round 'em up!

If your garden has ever fallen victim to the *Monolepta* beetle, you would have witnessed them arriving in swarms to devour the foliage of an unsuspecting tree or shrub. To trap them, take a white bucket, half-fill it with water and place it near the plants being attacked. The beetles are attracted to white (you will see them landing on white clothes on the clothes line) and will land in the bucket and drown.

Greg Morris, Woodview, NSW

Fooled again

An old bloke who lived at a very special place on the Hawkesbury River called Wondabyne passed on this valuable gardening idea. While handing me a bunch of his broccoli seedlings he said, 'If you don't want cabbage moth to attack these plants, place some egg shells around the place, including on the top of more developed plants. When the moth flies over looking for a spot to lay her eggs, she'll be tricked into thinking it's too crowded with other moths and she'll go elsewhere.'

Rose Hand, Lismore, NSW

SAP SUCKERS

Clean up

Dettol diluted with water at a rate of 1:10 makes an effective spray for getting rid of scale. It worked wonders on my camellias.

Christine Alexander, Clunes, NSW

Bromeliad scale

If you have scale on your bromeliads, don't use white oil. Bromeliads are extremely sensitive, and the oil can burn the leaves and kill them. Instead, use soapy water or a soap spray.

Judith Beavis, Suffolk Park, NSW

Sudsy solution

A simple soap spray will help control many different pests, like aphids, leafhoppers, whitefly and baby bronze orange bugs. To make it at home, dissolve 1–2 tablespoons liquid soap (not detergent) in 1 litre water, give it a good shake and then spray. If you like, add a few magic herbs and spices. Toss a handful of, say, garlic, onion, horseradish root, ginger root, rhubarb leaves or chillies into a container, cover with boiling water, seal and leave overnight. Strain it and add the liquid to your soap spray. If you don't use it immediately, you can freeze it for later.

A Drummond, Capalaba, Qld

A fishy tale

The nutrient content of fish-based fertilisers varies from one brand to another, as does the amount of fish oil they contain. Fish oil is an effective insecticide and miticide (substance for killing mites, ticks etc). A film of oil suffocates hidden pests. This explains why there is often a decline in numbers of mites, aphids, scale and other insects following regular foliar applications of fish-based products. Apply the fish fertiliser with a click-on hose applicator, directing the spray to the underside of the foliage, where insects often hide. A residue of oil on the surface of leaves also makes the foliage of treated plants look shiny and healthier.

Annette McFarlane, Brisbane, Qld

Goodbye whitefly

Harmful sap-sucking whitefly insects often gather on the undersides of the leaves of tomatoes and ornamentals. They feel protected there. Builder's insulation has a shiny reflective surface. If you lay some on the ground beneath your plants, the reflection disturbs the whiteflies, and they leave. Use rocks or pegs to secure the material.

George Thompson, Ferny Grove, Qld

Fly trap

Sap-sucking whitefly are attracted to the colour yellow. You can make a very effective whitefly trap with a yellow ice-cream container. Just smear it with petroleum jelly and the fly will stick to it.

Brian Green, Homebush, NSW

ANTS

Keeping ants at bay

To stop ants from going up my lemon tree to farm the scale, I place a small branch from the laurel tree (bay leaf) at the base. The ants leave and never return.

Sophie Martyn, Wonthaggi, Vic

Stick 'em up

Have you seen ants moving up and down the stems of your plants? Ants like to feed on the honeydew produced by sap-sucking insects like scale and they help to increase the population of scale by transporting their young to new locations. A great way to stop ants farming scale is to rub petroleum jelly around the trunk of your plants. The ants can't get past the sticky jelly. The good thing is that you only need one application because oily jelly won't wash off in the rain.

Barbara Waters, Murwillumbah, NSW

It's all white

If you have a problem with ants making mounds betweens pavers and in cracks of concrete, mix up some talcum powder and white pepper and tip into the cracks. They'll soon get the picture.

Cheryl Maggs, Bundaberg, Qld

DISEASES

Good hygiene

Good hygiene is an important strategy for reducing the destructive effects of petal blight disease in azaleas. I use a vacuum cleaner set on low suction to remove diseased flowers before the spores drop to the soil. The vacuum cleaner bag can then be dumped straight into the rubbish bin.

Claire Rowlands, Winston Hills, NSW

Multipurpose bleach

Bleach is a remarkably handy thing to have around the garden. Mixed according to directions, I have used a solution of bleach to scrub roses and rid them of scale and to cure an apple tree which had more than half of its stump eaten away by rot. Do take care not to splash it about too much.

Michael Yonwin, Thorneside, Qld

NATURE'S WAY

Weapons down

Don't kill off the good guys. A ladybird eats 400 aphids a week, but because her babies look like minute caterpillars, they get sprayed. Imagine how many aphids would be demolished if ladybirds could reach adulthood?

Beverley Morgan, Shepparton, Vic

Healthy plants — no pests

An outbreak of pests on your plants is nature's way of recycling plants that are not healthy. It's a good indication that the growing conditions for the plant are less than optimal. As a long-term solution to your pest problem, read up on the plant and check whether you're providing the best conditions. When conditions are right, plants seem less attractive to pests and better able to cope with minor pest invasions.

Chris Piechowicz, St Albans, Vic

Natural balance

Many people work hard to create gardens that are a haven for birds, lizards and butterflies. Butterflies produce baby caterpillars; gardeners spray caterpillars to protect foliage; and birds eat the sprayed caterpillars. Think about it?

Beverley Morgan, Shepparton, Vic

Good companion

We never use any sprays in our garden. Throughout the entire garden we plant garlic plants and we don't get many insects eating the veggies.

Maria-Anna Barry, Leyburn, Qld

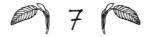

7

Animal-proofing your garden

Most animals are welcome in the garden; some of us have pets that we love to watch in the garden, while others spend a lot of time designing and building their gardens to make them more attractive to native fauna. But when animals start digging up our seedlings, nibbling at our roses and taking great chomps out of our paw paws, our attitudes are far less forgiving.

Gardeners all over Australia, from the suburbs to the bush, have stories to tell about unwelcomed intrusions from our furry friends. Thankfully, many have come up with clever suggestions on how to deal with some of the visiting critters.

POSSUMS

Popping possums

If troublesome possums are nibbling your plants, try securing some plastic bubble wrap around the stems. When the possums pierce a bubble, it POPS! This frightens them and they run away. If your plant is too small for wrapping the stem, secure some bubble wrap flat on the ground around the plant, using tent pegs.

Debbie Waters, Little Mountain, Qld

One in the net

I have had ongoing battles with possums eating my potted herbs. So recently I grouped the pots together and covered the lot with bird netting. It looks like I have finally won!

Karen Bittner, Olinda, Vic

CATS AND DOGS

Uncool for cats

To deter cats, sprinkle naphthalene flakes around the parts of your garden you don't want them to go. They don't like the smell of citrus peel, either, so whenever you eat an orange, try placing the peel in strategic locations.

Noeleen Ridgway, Ringwood North, Vic

Doggone it

Do neighbourhood dogs choose your garden, your special plants and your pots as the only places to pee? Try planting or rubbing the areas you want to protect with sprigs of a strange-smelling plant called dog bane (*Plectranthus ornatus* syn. *Coleus canis*). Dogs don't like it.

Beverley Morgan, Shepparton, Vic

BIRDS

Strawberries and cream

To keep birds from picking my strawberries, I push the fruiting stem inside a cut-down milk carton and place a small rock at the end to help hold it in place.

Frances Durdin, Port Elliot, SA

Mulch guard

As I swept back the mess of mulch the birds had scratched all over my drive, I thought of a simple and inexpensive way to deal with the problem. There was a roll of gutter mesh in the shed. Using timber pegs, I used the mesh to erect a barrier along the edge of the garden beds. Then I found some discarded welding rods at the recycle centre: an ideal long-term replacement for the timber pegs. Old tent pegs would be another good option. Simply thread the rods or pegs through the mesh and hammer into the ground. Mine has been in place now for over 10 years and works beautifully.

Janet Headlam, Launceston, Tas

Scary insects rule

To keep swallows and willy wagtails from nesting on your veranda, hang some scary metal marble-eyed 'insects' from the eaves. You can pick them up from discount stores for around $4 each. They twist, sway and flash in the breeze, which deters the birds. It's incredibly effective!

Angela Sole, Guyra, NSW

Snakes alive

If you want to keep hungry birds out of your fruit trees, try hanging some rubber snakes in them to scare them away. You can buy them cheaply from the toy section of bargain shops.

Tony Wootton, Maleny, Qld

It's in the bag

To keep birds from attacking your tomatoes, place each cluster of tomatoes inside paper lunch bag and fasten on with a clothes peg. It'll keep grubs and fruit fly out. Just look inside the bag from time to time to see when your tomatoes are ready to pick.

Mrs Pam Murison, Vermont, Vic

Chicken run

I used to have problems with my chooks escaping their pen. They always jumped on top of the gate and from there into my veggie patch. I found some old plastic bottles, slit them down the sides and laid them across the top of the gate. Now they can't get a grip on the curvy plastic surface, and my garden is saved. Ha ha.

Yolanda, Frankston, Vic

Watch it squirt

If bush turkeys are invading your garden, give them a squirt with a hose or a 'super soaker' water pistol. They won't come back a second time!

Elizabeth Crennan, Ocean Shores, NSW

OTHER CREATURES

Wallabies won't touch

If wallabies plague you in your garden, try planting lots of tomato plants in among the plants you want to protect. We have found they don't like the smell.

Michelle Harder, Nabiac, NSW

Out-foxed

Hungry menacing foxes were getting into my chook shed and sampling my prized hens. Foxes can't climb ladders, so I built a ladder system going in and out of the top of the chook shed. It took a few months to teach the chooks, but with a bit of patience it has worked like a charm. Now I can have a life and not worry about coming home before dark to check on my girls. In addition, I've built a little balcony at the top of the shed. Some nights, during the hot summer, I've spotted a few of them enjoying staying out on it.

Yolanda, Frankston, Vic

Rubber barrier

If you stack a couple of old tyres around your trees and shrubs this will stop hares attacking them.

Richard Cox, Blacksnake, Qld

Fort Knox — everybody out!

Where I garden, everything with feathers or legs wants to invade my veggie patch. One day, I had finally had enough. I decided I needed to build an impenetrable compound so that I could enjoy my passion. Now my entire veggie patch is fenced with second-hand chicken wire. Large animals, like horses and cows, can't reach over to partake in my leafy greens. The mesh goes over the top so it keeps the birds out, too. I've dug some old roofing iron into the soil around the base of the fence. That stops foxes and rabbits from invading. Then the gate has been fitted with spring hinges to stop dogs from opening it, and the chooks can't enter uninvited, either. You can almost see the lot of them peering in at my marvellous produce.

Terese Bock, Seymour, Vic

Weed control

Weeds are the recurring nightmare of every gardener. Some of us spend more time pulling weeds than doing any other job in the garden.

Experienced Australian gardeners have come up with a wealth of weed-control ideas, from how to use commercial herbicides safely and effectively to how to make useful home brews in the kitchen that don't cost the earth. Every one is sure to save you years of hard labour.

Tea tannin inhibitor

Instead of pouring your old tealeaves down the sink, top up the pot with cold water and pour it on your garden. The tannins in the tea seem to inhibit the germination of weed seeds. In the veggie patch, I concentrate on the same spot for a few days before shifting to another. It seems to help a lot, especially when I don't have time for pulling weeds.

Sandra Alderton, Cobram, Vic

Salty spray

Dissolve 1 cup salt in a little hot water, then add 4 litres vinegar and 9 drops dishwashing liquid. Use as a spray or paint it on your weeds. It's very effective.

A Drummond, Capalaba, Qld

Algae killer

Make up a deep pink solution of Condy's crystals (permanganate of potash), using 30g (1 tablespoon) to 4 litres of water, and pour it over concrete to kill moss and algae.

Noeleen Ridgway, Ringwood North, Vic

Weed and feed

To kill weeds, many gardeners sprinkle them with highly soluble high-nitrogen fertilisers, like urea and sulphate of ammonia. I find it easier and more efficient to apply it in a liquid form. I mix it up with water to make a strong solution — as strong as possible — then spray it onto the weeds in sunny weather. It's totally effective against bindii, white root and even flat weeds in the lawn, and will only kill the weeds that you make direct contact with.

Michael Yonwin, Thorneside, Qld

Working like steam

My heart it bleeds at the thought of people weeding 'twixt the paving.
This job can change a gardener from cool and calm to raving!
You scrape and scratch (and ache) your way along each paving row
While mentally telling every weed exactly where to go.
But there's a simple remedy my mother's mother taught her,
Drown each pesky little weed with steaming boiling water.
The weeds will quickly fade and die; they dry out and go brown.
And then it is a simple thing to casually lean down
And whisk out all those little weeds from in the paving cracks.
And it is such an easy job, it will not break your back.
So when weeds between the cracks grow up in fine tall fettle,
Do not groan and tear your hair — just go put on the kettle.

Helen Brumby, Rose Bay, Tas

Couch grass control

This is a great way to kill couch grass that has run wild in among your plants. Cut the top and bottom off a soft-drink bottle, place the upside-down bottle over the runners, pull as much of the couch as you can into it, and then spray inside the bottle. You coat the couch well without weedkiller drifting on other plants. It is often best to leave the bottle over the weed until the spray has dried. It works beautifully.

June Stanbrough, Blackburn South, Vic

Hits the mark

This is a simple and efficient way for killing weeds in paving, lawns and garden beds where you have to be careful not to spray weedkillers on sensitive plants. Take an old plastic drink bottle and put a pinhole in the lid. Fill the bottle with your solution of weedkiller and replace the lid. A bit of gentle pressure will direct a fine stream of the solution right onto the target, a bullseye every time. It's excellent for dandelions and oxalis in lawns.
Jack Bice, Lennox Head, NSW

Magic carpet

Whenever I'm sowing rows of vegetables like carrots, Asian greens, beans or whatever, between the rows I lay down a cut-to-width strip of carpet. This gives me a weed-free bed from planting right through to harvesting and it helps to hold in the moisture, too. The strips of carpet last for many seasons.
Marjorie Bligh, Devonport, Tas

No weed hang-ups

I hate weeding but I still combat weeds in my veggie patch. One of my favourite methods is to recycle old telephone directories: I tear out the pages and place them around the base of my plants or any areas I want to keep weed-free, then I water well. This keeps the weeds down and keeps the worms happy.
Kerrie Goodchild, Derby, WA

Clean weeding

When you're pulling weeds, don't leave them sitting around in piles on the ground. It's a great way to spread the seed about. Put them straight into a bucket, garbage bin or similar. Why don't you use two containers? One for seed heads and persistent culprits, like nutgrass, and one for the weeds that are destined for the compost.

Barbara Benham, Stanthorpe, Qld

Weeds in pavers

After spending many backbreaking hours trying to rid a large paved area of weeds, I found that a light application of common salt was a pretty good control method. My partner made me a handy contraption for applying it without having to bend. It's a funnel attached to a long hollow tube.

Daisy Cybinski, The Gap, Qld

Very merry weeding

The best way to get rid of weeds organically is to heed the advice given by Father Christmas every year: Hoe, hoe, hoe!

Peter McCallum, Booleroo, SA

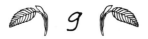

Tips from the top

When we set about compiling *Garden Guru II*, we asked some of Australia's most respected celebrity gardeners to recall the time when they realised they were hopelessly hooked on gardening. We also invited them to share a favourite tip — one that has been passed on to them by an influential gardener in their lives.

I hope you enjoy their delightful stories as much as we have.

NEW SOUTH WALES

Phil Dudman
ABC North Coast, Lismore

As a teenager growing up in Brisbane, I had this incredible urge to rip everything out of my parents' garden and replant it. I spent a lot of time in the garden then. One of my jobs was to mow. I loved to experiment with different heights on the mower, creating all sorts of patterns in the turf to make it look like Lord's Cricket Ground or something. I even mowed my backyard cricket pitch extra short and would drag the old man out to bowl at me. On weekends, I enjoyed visiting nurseries with my mother. Natives were all the rage in the 1970s, and I felt drawn to their unique flowers and foliage textures. I took great delight in planting grevilleas, bottlebrush, banksias, westringeas and kangaroo paw throughout the garden, welcoming the local wildlife that visited from then on. Even mistakes had positive aspects. My first lesson in what to plant where came from watching the Geraldton wax fail dismally during a wet Queensland summer.

Tip: One of the most valuable tips passed on to me was from a fellow teacher I worked with at TAFE, Peter Newman. I was also landscaping then, and often complained of a bad back after a day of digging. Peter suggested that the common method of using a spade in the middle of your stance is really bad for your back. If you keep the spade on the outside of your stance and use the outside of your foot to push the blade into the soil, you can keep your back straight and dig all day without any strain. It's made a load of difference. Peter received this piece of wisdom from an elderly gentleman he met one day.

Judy Horton
702 ABC Sydney

It happened when I was about 6 years old. One day we went to Luna Park, Sydney's famous fun park, with its merry-go-rounds, slides, clowns and everything else that *should* bring joy to a child's heart. But I still remember the thud of disappointment I felt as I walked through the legendary laughing face at the entrance. I'd expected to find myself in a beautiful park, but this was not at all the case. I must have been the only child there who was crestfallen because Luna Park didn't have lots of trees, rolling lawns and flowerbeds! Looking back now, I realise I was destined to be involved in gardening.

When I was busy establishing my first garden as an adult, I used to visit a keen elderly gardener who told me that, for her, gardening had been a lifelong journey, and her ideas had evolved over time. To start with, she'd made traditional, colour-filled plantings, then she became obsessed with native plants and the clever ways they adapted themselves to their environment. At the time, I couldn't see beyond large showy flowers but now I am far more interested in the subtleties of native plants, too. Though Phyllis is long gone, I think of her often. Edna Walling made a similar journey in her gardening life.

Helen Young
702 ABC Sydney

I learnt my love of gardening from my mother and through helping my parents while they gardened on weekends, from the time I was quite small. They must have realised I was hooked on gardening when they dug up a section of lawn to make me my very own patch where I could grow the flowers I loved. I still remember the sweet fragrance of stocks in the winter and how fascinating it was to peel open the fat buds of poppies, unfolding their silky petals to discover the colour of each. In fact I still do it!

> Tip: I don't know whose grandma first said it, but the old adage, 'One year's seeds, seven years weeds', is the simplest piece of garden advice I know. Don't let a few weeds become hundreds — if you're too busy to pull them out, at least snap off the flower heads when you see them, before they can form seeds. You'll save yourself a huge amount of work later on.

Margaret Sirl
ABC South East, Bega

My passion for plants began when I was a very small child. I seemed to always have a flower clutched in my hand. Fortunately my parents both enjoyed gardening and encouraged my interest. Memories of dad encouraging me to 'help' plant his vegetable seedlings and allowing me to 'gently' water them in will remain with me always.

Norm was our neighbour and a great gardener. He made a powerful, smelly brew from seaweed, fish 'bits', herbs and weeds. After a month of brewing in a covered drum, it was diluted with water and poured around his plants. They glowed with good health and vigour.

Tip: Many years ago a very wise gardener said to me, 'What comes out of the ground must go back in.' This saying had had a lasting impression on me as soil fed well with decomposed organic matter rewards abundantly.

Sean O'Brien
1233 ABC Newcastle

I was a bit of a latecomer when it came to discovering my love of gardening. I always wanted to be a marine biologist but I can't swim, so that idea went out the window. Instead I went on to university to become a farmer. That didn't work out, so I decided to take up horticulture. But it wasn't until I owned my own home, where I designed and built my first garden, that the gardening bug really struck. It's so deeply satisfying when you start with nothing and create a garden you enjoy every day.

> Tip: The most valuable thing I have learnt is to ignore the rules and try something different. Even if I was told, 'You can't grow that there,' or 'You can't plant this with that', I still did it! Sometimes it didn't work, but I had fun doing it anyway. Plants are very adaptable, and if you have the time and patience, my advice is, 'Experiment — rules are meant to be broken!'

John Gabriele
ABC Illawarra, Wollongong

For me, the seeds of lifelong gardening were sown when I was a young sprout of 10 years old. At school, if I completed my class work with diligence, my friends and I were allowed to tend the school gardens — a fantastic way of getting out of lessons! I remember being very proud of my first 'landscape construction'. It consisted of weeding a narrow strip of garden bed outside our classroom and laying some old bricks on edge at 45 degrees. My teacher, Mr Ted Elphic, may not have realised the real lesson he was teaching us … or did he?

> Tip: I have learnt many lessons through gardening. Your environment will tell you everything you need to know. Our own lives are staged in a similar fashion to the life played out daily in our gardens. There is everything from birth, growth, courtship, love, sickness, death and rebirth. The open mind and the open heart will connect with nature and find meaning.

Pam Albutt
ABC Mid North Coast, Port Macquarie

I have the fondest memories of my first job, which was working with Arthur Fairall, the Superintendent of Kings Park Botanic in Western Australia, in 1968. An avid collector of Australian plants, Arthur imparted a tremendous enthusiasm for our extraordinary flora. We would go on field trips recording cultivation notes as well as collecting seeds and propagating material from plants in the wild. I formed a deep admiration for our delightful wildflowers with their varied forms and colours, their ability to survive the most difficult conditions and their informality, which is quintessentially Australian. This early introduction to our unique flora has left me hooked for life. I still prefer the wonderful casual style of native gardens to the sculptural, repetitive gardens that are currently in vogue.

Tip: The most valuable advice I can offer is take time to observe your garden. When you stroll past your plants, you see when they are thirsty or hungry and you can act promptly when some voracious insect is devouring them! Nothing is more calming than stopping to pull out a weed or stumbling across a plant that's suddenly in flower.

Malcolm McKinlay
1233 ABC Newcastle

My passion for gardening grew as I did, nurtured by people dear to me. During my early childhood, I spent hours in my Nan's garden, working and observing. She was a highly resourceful gardener on a limited budget, growing vegetables and flowers from seed and taking cuttings of whatever she could. With these lessons, she taught me the foundations of gardening.

I was also inspired by my mother and the way she greened our unit with potted plants, and by a kind headmaster who allowed me to plant and maintain my primary school's gardens. He gave me space and purpose. Even then, I probably knew I would tread a career path of gardening.

Tip: My Pop would always say to add cow manure to the soil when the flowers and vegetables are finished to reward the soil. Soil is like the foundation of a house. Get it right and gardening should be easier and more rewarding.

Reg Kidd
ABC Central West, Orange

From a young age, I was keen on travelling in the bush to places like Bourke, Louth, Broken Hill and Menindee. My love of 'all things growing' meant that agriculture and botany became my favourite subjects at school. On school holidays, I worked on various horticultural enterprises in my beloved Central West region. Naturally, I went on to study Agricultural Science at uni, then followed a career in teaching agriculture, horticulture and natural resources. My greatest mentor (and hero) was Bob Gastoe, a great icon of the sheep industry who had an uncanny knowledge of the bush, plants and their relationships. I travelled extensively with him and it 'flamed' the passion.

> Tip: The most important tip I can pass on is get to know growing media, whether it's potting mix or the in-situ soil in your paddocks or backyard. Understanding its texture and pH and modifying it where necessary can lead to endless joy from successful gardening.

Warren Sheather

ABC New England North West, Tamworth

My passion for gardening, especially native plant cultivation, began when I married my wife, Gloria. She was already interested in native plants and was the catalyst for this lifelong obsession.

Tip: I have found that close observation of nature is the key to understanding plants and their needs. Early in our marriage, my wife and I visited a national park near Sydney. It was there I realised that native plants like to grow close together. This has influenced the way we garden with native plants. We position plants very close to each other, and use many diverse varieties. In this way, we have cultivated a wide range of natives that thrive in a relatively hostile environment.

Helen Whalen
1233 ABC Newcastle

My father had a nursery on the side of a very steep hill. As soon as I could walk, I would tag along after Scamp, the dog, who followed my father everywhere. By the age of 3, I had my own section in a glasshouse, where I grew cuttings and propagated seeds. I am now in my youthful old age and still my greatest pleasure, other than my grandchildren, is designing beautiful gardens and passing on the knowledge I have acquired.

Tip: One of the best things I have learnt is that to have a happy and healthy garden, you must feed it well. Fish emulsion is excellent. Feed your plants regularly with it by pouring a solution all over the foliage and root zone. This builds up the immune system of the plant and also helps to protect it from an attack of pests or diseases. I feel that the oil in fish emulsion puts a protective sheen over the leaves, making it difficult for insects and spores to attach to the plant.

Adrian Podmore
ABC Riverina, Wagga Wagga

I have fond childhood memories of tending the garden flowers and vegetables with my grandparents and family. They passed on a valuable understanding and passion for gardening and horticulture in general. It's wonderful to watch plants grow and reach their potential as you nurture and maintain the conditions for their growth cycle. I especially love growing trees. They are the backbone of any garden, which will be there for decades to come.

Tip: Take time to plant some veggies. You will always be rewarded for your efforts. If you see a weed, pull it out! It's much easier than having to weed a whole garden. If you must spray to control pests and diseases in the garden, try using one of the more environmentally friendly sprays available now. Use mulches on your gardens to conserve water and suppress weed growth; it frees you up for other garden activities as well. Sow seeds or take cuttings of plants; it's much cheaper than buying seedlings or small plants. To be more water-wise in the garden, grow plants suited to your climate and local environment.

Jackie Battaglini
ABC Mid North Coast, Port Macquarie

Tip: Broad beans are an excellent crop to grow in rotation with tomatoes. Plant them in the cooler months, when tomatoes won't grow. When you've finished harvesting the beans, dig the plants into the soil. They make a wonderful green manure, enriching the soil with nutrients and organic matter.

VICTORIA

John Patrick
Victorian Presenter, ABC Gardening Australia TV

I started gardening with a wooden spade when I was very young, growing up in the UK. Our neighbour was a world authority on gladioli and I 'helped' him in his garden. He grew his plants in rows all of the same variety, his wife noting in pencil what corm and how many of them went into each row. She kept meticulous records. I liked to dig up a corm here and there and replant it in the wrong position and thus developed my creative gardening streak! Evidence of my success could be seen in summer when a gorgeous white spike erupted among the mauves or a giant orange among the delicate butterflies!

My neighbour showed his gladioli stems at the Chelsea and Southport Shows. Damaged flowers and those that didn't make the grade were cast, half-dead, onto the compost heap. I rescued them to have my own flower shows, displaying half-dead glads until the very last flower on the spike died. By this time the water smelt, the stems were slimy, and my parents had developed a loathing for gladioli that I now share as an adult!

Tip: The best gardening advice I ever got was from my father, 'For God's sake, get those bloody stinky gladioli stems OUTSIDE!'

Carolyn Blackman
774 ABC Melbourne

I became involved in gardening through my grandparents, Frank and Enid. I spent nearly every weekend of my childhood learning about gardening by osmosis from them in Ballarat, Victoria.

Tip: Ask your soil! Gardeners usually notice plant problems through the appearance of the foliage, and a frequent knee-jerk reaction is to employ more TLC. This usually comes in the form of extra watering, just in case, and a big dose of whichever fertiliser happens to be in the shed. In many situations, much can be learnt about a problem by digging a trowel-depth hole in the area close to the root ball. This immediately alerts you to fundamental problems such as overly dry soils or poor drainage. In either case, a dose of fertiliser will usually exacerbate the problem! It is by far better to focus on soil health and structure than instant 'remedies'. As a general rule, only fertilise actively growing plants that are reasonably healthy.

Kevin Walsh
ABC Central and Northern Victoria

My very first garden was a small patch along the back paling fence in our suburban garden in Melbourne. It ran from one fencepost to the next, and although it was only 15cm (6 inches) wide, to me it was the whole world. My mum prepared the soil, and together we planted a row of flowers from a punnet. I remember the sun on my back, the bright white roots, the feel of the soil and the sense of expectation. I was 5 years of age!

Tip: Here's an easy-to-make general-purpose organic pesticide you might like to try. Pour 1 teaspoon eucalyptus oil, 1 teaspoon liquid detergent and 500mL water into an atomiser. Shake well and spray to control insect pests such as aphids, small caterpillars, whiteflies, and pear and cherry slugs. It's important to spray the pests themselves, so make sure you get it under the leaves, if that's where they are.

Beverley Morgan
ABC Goulburn Murray, Wodonga

After our first year of marriage, in the week leading up to his birthday, I gave my husband a present every day. His gift for Day 3 was a propagation box. After I explained to him what it was, both of us became hooked — me because I already loved plants; Lindsay because he loved the idea of creating plants for nothing. From that, 35 years in the horticultural industry followed. I'm still hooked on both the husband and plants.

> Tip: I don't believe that anybody is ever a bad gardener. Like all things, knowledge comes with trial and error. Above all, just be interested in gardening. The rest will follow. And there's no age limit when sharing the joy of gardening.

Nancy Morgan
ABC Gippsland, Sale

Growing up in the Californian Mojave Desert, my idea of gardening was dragging cacti around with a 4-wheel drive! However, when I came to Australia a love affair with gardening and this country began. Luckily, I met my mentor, Patricia Crooke. She taught me many things like nomenclature and, for want of a better word, the 'forensics' of the garden. With her help and support, I've had a nursery since 1981. My love affair with Australia and gardening continues, and I'm gobsmacked daily to think how lucky I am to live here.

Tip: Every guest in my nursery has a hint to share, all of them handy. Here are a couple of interesting remedies passed on by a Bedouin chemist who often relies on what's available. To treat a herpes-related affliction, like a cold sore, dot it with a blob of white sap from the end of a fresh cutting of a fig. You shouldn't get one again. And try this for acne. With your thumbnail, split the main vein of a fig leaf and dot the liquid on affected skin. Leave for a while before washing it off.

Harry Benyon
ABC Goulburn Murray, Wodonga

In 22 years as a retail nurseryman, this is one of the funniest complaints I've had. One day, a lady came into the nursery quite angry. Some months before, she had purchased a tree fern and planted it in her garden. When the plant began to grow, the fronds came from ground level and there was no sign of any growth from the top. I took her over to the fresh tree ferns we had in stock and asked her to show me how she had planted it. She pointed to the top of the tree fern, where the fresh fronds were about to unfurl, and she said, 'I put those roots in the ground.' She had put the plant in upside down. The message behind this story is always put the green side up!

QUEENSLAND

Colin Campbell
Queensland Presenter, ABC Gardening Australia TV

Tip: Immediately after sowing seeds, mix up a fifth of a teaspoon of Epsom salts in a litre of water and wet the seed-raising mix or soil with this solution. The magnesium contained in the Epsom salts activates the enzymes that break down the food supply for the newly emerging plant, and as a result you get quicker and better germination.

Annette McFarlane
612 ABC Brisbane

My grandparents were terrific gardeners. Our family lived with my grandparents until I started school, so I have always attributed my love of gardening to them. I still recall the way my grandfather would make up a magic liquid mixture (which I later discovered was liquid manure) and apply it with ceremony to his vegetables. It certainly worked. He grew rhubarb as thick as your wrist. Ferns were my grandmother's passion. She had a fernery at the rear of the house filled with superb maidenhair. I have never been able to grow anything nearly as grand.

Tip: Everybody expects garden writers and television presenters to have spectacular gardens, but no-one I know would be prepared to put their garden 'on show' — well, at least not without quite a bit of work! It doesn't matter whether you are the neat and tidy type who likes perfectly manicured lawns or have a more relaxed style whereby plants do their own thing. When it comes to gardening, the most important thing is to get out there and enjoy yourself. Most of us garden for our own pleasure. If others enjoy our gardens, that is just an extra bonus.

Rod Hultgren
ABC Southern Queensland, Toowoomba

Early success in gardening is so important. I can remember when I became keen on gardening at about 7 years old. Someone gave me a packet of 'White Icicle' radish seed. I think they all germinated and grew quickly. Every day after school I enjoyed pulling, washing and eating these mild radishes. I also enjoyed being (as I thought at the time) a great and successful gardener. I was hooked.

Tip: I really was the worst maker of compost this side of the black stump. I'd read all the books on how to make perfect plant food. But what I was taking out of the compost heap was almost in the same condition it was when added to the heap. Nowhere in the books was it mentioned that the heap had to be turned. Luckily a friend came to the rescue and suggested it should be turned once a week. After doing just that on a regular basis, I now make compost *almost* good enough to eat (if I were a plant).

Penny McKinlay
ABC Southern Queensland, Toowoomba

People who love being outside, getting physical, combining colours and watching things grow become gardeners. They are a special breed. Those of us who garden in the heavy black soils of the Darling Downs in southern Queensland have to have something extra. Here we grow good wheat, barley and cotton … and weeds, but anything else is a major effort!

The pH of the soil is 9. During droughts, cracks up to 30cm wide appear; and when wet, it's a cement mix. Consequently, you have to spread gypsum at the rate of 1kg per metre; barrow in truckloads of soil, sand, manure and leaf mould; and build beds a minimum of 400mm above the soil level. Mulch is used by the ton.

Temperatures drop to minus 8°C in winter and go up to 41°C in summer. Winds blow in from all directions, and the bore water is hard.

So what can we grow? Many native plants fail, so we turn to the big old English trees, as well as Chinese, Korean and Spanish varieties. Cutting-grown roses and tough perennials do very well.

For a good while it's forgotten to rain, and the commodity prices for crops are not sparkling, but we're still here and we're still gardening. We love it and we wouldn't be anywhere else.

Sonja Anderson
ABC Far North, Cairns

Tip: Spectacular tropical blooms like heliconias, costus and gingers are highly valued for their magnificent and colourful bracts. They make wonderful cut flowers. Once cut, however, they draw little water through their stems and need a humid microclimate around them to maximise their vase life. The day before cutting them from your garden, water the plants well. Cut the stems just before dawn. At this point, the plant is losing hardly any moisture by transpiration, and the cell walls of the bracts will be most turgid. After cutting (or if you have purchased blooms from a florist), soak the entire stem in a tub or sink of clear water at room temperature for an hour or so. If the stem and flower are too big for your sink, then submerge the bract and as much of the stem as possible or use your bathtub for larger blooms! You can put a touch of dishwashing detergent in the water so that the bract and stem are coated with a slight film, helping to slow evaporation from the cells. When you make your vase arrangement, also put in the vase the long-stemmed leaves of the plant. Spray the arrangement with water a couple of times a day — more often in an air-conditioned room. This will keep the microclimate around your tropical flowers as humid as possible. Change the vase water regularly and your beautiful display of tropical blooms will last much longer.

TASMANIA

Peter Cundall
Tasmanian Presenter, ABC Gardening Australia TV
ABC State-wide Tasmania

Tip: One of the most effective ways of controlling bracken fern weed is with a lawnmower. Summer is when these plants are in full, active growth, and cutting them right down to ground level has a massive weakening effect. The pulverised remains also make fantastic mulch. Do this 2 or 3 times in summer and that will put an end to your bracken fern problem.

Tip: Most European plums and gages should be left to hang-ripen in summer. Wastage often occurs when stone fruit are harvested while still hard, green and tasteless. They will not sugar-up, even as they soften. So be patient. Use your sense of smell and don't be afraid to give all stone fruit a gentle, friendly squeeze, just to make sure they are ready to be properly slurped. To ensure maximum rich, sweet flavour, some connoisseurs even wait until the skins have started to wrinkle a little.

Tip: Prickly plants, like cacti, are difficult to handle when re-potting. Roll up some newspaper; bend it around the spiny parts, leaving enough to create a handle; then grip firmly. This allows the plants to be lifted and moved around with ease — and complete safety.

Tip: Winter is always when lawns that are subjected to a lot pedestrian traffic start to show unsightly signs of wear and tear. It is an easy job to insert pre-cast concrete stepping-stones across areas that receive the most punishment. Place out on the grass a row of round or square flagstones — but only a few centimetres apart. Cut around them with an old knife. This allows the battered turf and soil below it to be lifted cleanly. Pack the base of each cavity with fine road-metal and adjust the flagstones so they sit just below soil level. They can be mown over and always look good.

Andrew Westwood
ABC Northern Tasmania, Launceston

I was a relative latecomer to the gardening scene but when I took on a job as a first-year parks and garden apprentice I became a devotee. After months of soil preparation with manure, compost, feeding and weeding, my first floral display came to life. Full of petunias, phlox, and Livingston daisies, it was an awe-inspiring experience. It made me realise the true beauty of the flowers and the way that their colour can bring life to an otherwise dull and lifeless landscape.

Tip: An old foreman of mine gave me some invaluable advice. Growing vegetables is a fine pastime for a young gentleman, he said, as long as you leave space for some flowers. As hard as you try, young women respond much better to flowers!

Greg Kerin
936 ABC Hobart

Tip: A listener from Howrah in Hobart once told me that if you have fungus that thrives in warm, moist conditions, then it's an indication that your soil is potash-deficient. This can be overcome by adding wood ash to the soil. Adding comfrey leaves or rotted seaweed is another method of correcting the deficiency. Or try making compost with fern leaves that have been removed in summer, when the potash is highest in the fronds.

Tip: Soils that contain very large proportions of organic matter are susceptible to becoming sour if they are heavily watered. Broken charcoal mixed through the soil will help prevent this acidic build-up. Crush thru charcoal into pieces, then mix through the soil and water in well. Charcoal is also helpful in seed trays or in a jar of water when striking cuttings, and in pot plants it aids drainage.

WESTERN AUSTRALIA

Josh Byrne
Western Australia Presenter, ABC Gardening Australia TV

For me it all started at the age of 14 with a 4m² no-dig veggie patch on top of the lawn out the back of the family home. I was fascinated by how a few bales of straw, a load of compost and a handful of seeds could be converted into bundles of fresh vegetables within a matter of months. This humble start triggered something special, and I have been replacing lawn with vegetables, fruit trees and natives ever since.

Tip: The heat generated from successful 'hot composting' will kill many plant diseases and some weed seeds but will not necessarily kill off bulbous weeds like onion grass and gladiolus or running grasses like couch. Soak these in a bucket of water with the lid on for several weeks so they rot, then the nutrient-rich slurry can be safely added to the compost bin without the risk of re-shooting.

Sabrina Hahn
ABC State-wide Western Australia and 'Overnights' with Trevor Chappell

At the tender age of 4, I would pinch my mother's baking trays and fill them with miniature gardens that I pillaged from my grandmother's garden. During those early formative years, I learnt that the garden was a magical place to reinvent oneself and the perfect setting to find peace and connect with nature.

Years later, I replaced cake tins with ink and paper to create garden designs, but I'm still known to prance about in fairy wings and I have an inexhaustible passion for plants and nature. I owe much of my intrinsic knowledge of plants to my mother and grandmother. They were exceptionally gifted gardeners with a wonderful eye for design and an abiding love of the Australian landscape.

Tip: One of my favourite tips came from my grandmother. Crutchings (or dags) from sheep make a wonderful all-in-one water retention and slow-release fertiliser. Put them in the bottom of your planting hole. The wool retains water and provides food for microorganisms. In heavy soils, the wool also assists with drainage. The poo provides nitrogen and potassium needed for plant growth.

Tip: One of my favourite personal discoveries: if you live near a brewery, the beer waste of yeast and hops makes a wonderful soil conditioner, and the worms devour it. It is fantastic to use in vegetable beds, and the yeast helps to repel sap-sucking insects. If nothing else, the garden smells fantastic on a hot summer's day and attracts friends from near and far.

SOUTH AUSTRALIA

Malcolm Campbell
891 ABC Adelaide

Tip: A few years ago, an elderly lady in Dulwich, Adelaide, showed me her collection of wisterias in pots. She was well into her 80s, and some of the pots were very large. When I asked her how she managed to re-pot them, she showed me a technique so simple, I'm staggered that it hasn't been demonstrated more widely. Using a bulb corer, you create a hole as deep as you can and remove the potting media in about 3–6 spots around the perimeter of the large pot. Into the cavity, you place a mixture of well-rotted compost laced with slow-release fertiliser, pressing it in and capping it off with some potting mix so that the cores don't dry out. It works a treat with maximum benefit for minimal effort and root disturbance.

Sophie Thomson
South Australia Presenter, Gardening Australia TV

I had an extraordinary childhood growing up with parents who owned a plant nursery and, most importantly, who had created a magnificent garden. Flowers, leaves, fruits and just about anything else you could grow were collected for delight, discovery, interest or purely to delight the imagination. The giant leaves of *Gunnera* were sewn together to make skirts for dress-ups: they attained rather grander proportions than those in the flower fairies poster on my wall.

> Tip: My mother was the first to tell me, 'One year's seeding is seven years' weeding.' Although I know it was not one of her originals, anyone who has ever let a weed seed in their garden will know this is true.

Calum Haygarth
ABC South East SA, Mount Gambier

Parsley, sage, raspberries and thyme. I was 3–4 years old, growing up in the UK, spending the balmy English summers in my grandmother's garden. It was full of colour, bordered by clipped privet hedges with the most amazing kitchen garden. I vividly recall the smell of thyme and the tonnes of raspberries! To this day, whenever I rub past some thyme oozing its pungent aroma, I think of her and her wonderful herb garden. As for the raspberries, I still miss the huge full bowl you could collect in minutes. They were grown with precision on specially constructed frames that enclosed the wayward canes. Tiny threads of sewing cotton were laced between the timber uprights. They had old foil milk bottle tops threaded through them so that they rattled uncontrollably in the breeze, scaring all the birds away from the fruit. It seemed crazy, but it worked!

Tip: The most valuable tip I have was passed on to me by The Queen Mother one day: 'IT'S ALL IN THE PREPARATION.' I began my horticultural career in the gardens of The Castle of Mey in the far north of Scotland. It was a holiday castle for Her Majesty Queen Elizabeth the Queen Mother. The vegetable garden was amazing, surrounded by huge stone walls designed to keep the harsh wind and elements at bay. There we produced more than enough produce for the Royal kitchen.

We made what they call leaf mould in the UK — compost basically. Painstakingly, in autumn, we would go around the entire castle grounds raking up all the autumn leaves into piles and transferring them to huge pens constructed of chicken wire. The pens were alongside one of the gigantic garden walls, and they went on for miles. When the leaf mould was ready, we would dig in the entire contents of the pens throughout the garden to give back all that had been depleted by the intensive growing.

John Menzel
ABC Riverland, Renmark

Tip: The dahlia season of 2005/06 saw some of the hottest conditions on record. Three days in a row the mercury reached 49°C under cover, yet we managed to grow our best dahlias ever in our production nursery. It's all due to adopting the 'pulse' watering system. We watered our dahlias 6 times per day for 10 minutes at a time. Drippers were spaced 300mm apart and were the type that could emit 2 litres per hour. It is generally accepted that dahlias are large users of water, but this is now challenged. We actually used 50 percent less water than normal during that excessively hot summer.

Ian Andrews
ABC Riverland, Renmark

Tip: It's often said that the more you learn about something, the more you realise there is to know! There's so much you can learn about the science of gardening that it can take the fun out of it: feeding programs, NPK balance, minerals, trace elements etc, etc. It's as though you need a chemistry degree to work it out. My tip: always change your fertiliser, and if necessary, buy supermarket specials. Each fertiliser is made up differently. By rotating what you use, you should cover all a plant's requirements. 'Green fingers are developed from dirty hands.'

NORTHERN TERRITORY

Darryl South
ABC Darwin 105.7FM

I was growing pumpkins when I was 5 years old; then the 'fruit fly men' from the Department of Agriculture came to take them away, a harsh lesson in pest eradication. Of course, I burst into tears. I guess that was the moment I realised I was addicted to gardening. I continued to grow vegetables, all the way through high school and agricultural college. I got involved in the nursery industry at the age of 16 and am still there today. I've never veered from that path in 46 years and I'm probably more committed now than ever. You never stop learning about plants. There is always something different to discover.

Tip: My agriculture teacher at school left me with lasting impressions. He was an Englishman named Bill Bailey. He taught me about observation. Looking carefully at a plant and noting its growing conditions will quickly reveal any problems. Remember, plants are living things, and they respond in much the same way as people and animals. Give your plants the right amount of water, light and nutrients and they will remain healthy.

Chris Nathanael
ABC Darwin 105.7FM

My father was a very keen gardener in Melbourne and had the entire front- and backyard planted with fruit trees and vegetables. There was much more than we could ever consume, so neighbours and visitors always left with fresh produce. My father's enthusiasm hadn't brushed off onto me until I went to live in Darwin in 1962. There I found accommodation with a couple in a newly built house. They were developing their garden, and I suggested a few fruit trees. The next day, they presented me with 4 fruit trees to plant. Well, from that time on I had 'caught the bug'. I started studying all manner of weird and wonderful fruit trees growing in the tropics, many of which were not yet available in Australia. There was a time when I would buy anything that fruited. Like the elephant apple — a fruit that I later discovered was a favourite of elephants and monkeys, not humans. It was all fun. Today we have over 200 different varieties of fruit in the orchard and we produce more than 400 varieties in our fruit tree nursery. I still can't wait for the sun to rise in the morning so that I can be among my fruit trees.

Leonie Norrington
Northern Territory presenter, ABC Gardening Australia TV

Tip: Tomatoes need to be staked or else they lay on the ground, where the fruit rots and the plants becomes a tangled mess of foliage, giving bugs and grubs a nice place to hide from butcher birds and other predators. Only problem is, in the Northern Territory stakes attract termites, and even when you tie branches with cloth or stockings, the weight of the fruit breaks the stems. So I always grow my tomatoes through old wire single-bed frames. One bed will support 8 plants. Put the bed over the seedlings and train the branches through the wire as they grow. Stringing some pig wire between 4 star pickets also works well as frame. You can fold the wire back and forth to make a couple of layers to support lanky breeds like cherry tomatoes.

Tip: Some people prune their tomatoes by picking out the side branches as they form. But my grandmother reckoned that creating open wounds on a healthy tomato plant is only inviting disease.

Flowers, trees, shrubs, and climbers

Flowers are the jewels that make the garden a special place. For many, it's the sheer beauty of flowers that has inspired their love of gardening and growing things.

When we called out for ideas from dedicated flower lovers, we were delighted by the response. There were many simple suggestions for helping your flowering plants bloom better and for longer.

Have a look then try some of them out for yourself.

Delightful dahlias

I grow dahlias for presenting at shows and here is something I do which promotes longer, stronger stems and better-quality blooms. It also encourages a longer flowering season. When they are large enough to handle, remove the buds and shoots beside the main bud. Also take off the shoots from the next couple of leaf joins. It's a technique that could be applied for a whole range of home-grown cut flowers.

Steven Wedd, Murwillumbah, NSW

Coffee lovers

Leftover coffee grounds do wonders for azalea and camellia bushes. In alkaline soils they help lower the pH and act as a food source for soil microorganisms.

Sabrina Hahn, WA [QUERY: Suburb?]

Always looking good

Tulips and other bulbs make a terrific seasonal display in the garden, but if you want to save the bulbs for the next season, you have to wait until the tops have died down naturally. That way, the bulbs can store the energy they need to do it all again. Problem is, they can look quite unsightly in the garden for a long time after their big show. If this bothers you, try what I do. I plant my bulbs in containers before burying them in the garden. After the show, I lift them and place them out of sight while they complete their cycle. That way, I can use the space to plant flowering annuals for the summer. Use a good-quality potting mix with some cow manure added and once they are showing growth, feed fortnightly with liquid fertiliser.

Betty Dent, Wentworth Falls, NSW

Grow your own trellis

If you like to grow giant sunflowers, as I do, then you might try this. Don't dig the plants out when they are finished at the end of summer. Plant your sweet pea seeds among them in autumn. The sweet peas will climb happily up and around the rough trunks and stems of the sunflower plants, saving you the trouble of erecting a trellis for them. Just cut the flower heads off the sunflowers so they stand up straight. You could also grow beans, peas or snow peas.

Wendy De Burgh, Castle Forbes Bay, Tas

Rose tonic

Every spring, I treat my roses with a diluted molasses solution. It seems to give them extra strength and vitality and I no longer have problems with pests like aphids or diseases like black spot. Dissolve ? cup molasses in hot water then mix with sufficient cold water to fill a 9-litre watering can. This is enough to treat 3 rose bushes. Pour it all over the fresh spring foliage and around the root zone.

Mary Blechyndon, Beverley, WA

pH change for the better

My roses never seemed to thrive until I read that they prefer a pH of around 6.5–6.8. I did a test on my soil and found that the pH was a low 5. So I applied some lime to raise the pH and check it regularly to see if I need more. What a difference it has made, and now I enjoy a bounty of blooms.

Mark Smith, Holland Park, Qld

Healthy hands

When you've finished working in your rose garden, wash your hands with methylated spirits. This will help stop infection and take away any stinging from prickly thorns.

Margaret Mitchell, Kyogle, NSW

Blooming bougainvilleas

If you're growing bougainvillea in a pot, don't be tempted to re-pot it unless you really must. Bougainvillea blooms best when it's pot-bound. You can leave it in its original pot right up to the point when the roots have totally replaced all of the potting mix and you can't keep it watered any longer.

Vicki Cashin, Bronte, NSW

Good training

Climbers always have the habit of rushing upwards, leaving the bottom of the wall or fence looking bare. To overcome this, when it's young, train your climber to grow horizontally and low down.

Nola McRae, Wagga Wagga, NSW

Blooming brunfelsia

If you want to plant a brunfelsia (yesterday, today, tomorrow) in your garden, avoid placing it near a streetlight. It won't bloom if you do.

Colin Bradshaw, Bilambil Heights, NSW

Winter colour

Helleborus (or winter rose) flowers make a wonderful cut flower at a time of the year — winter — when there's little else. Always plunge the cut ends into boiling water before arranging them in the vase. To care for them in the garden, cut off the old leaves in late autumn and divide the plants in spring.

Nola McRae, Wagga Wagga, NSW

Found what I'm looking for

Every gardener needs a shade tree where they can sit and admire their beautiful garden during the warm months of the year. I've been searching for my perfect tree and I think I've finally found it. It is the very beautiful *Magnolia grandiflora* 'Exmouth', a gorgeous, spreading evergreen tree with large, fragrant, creamy white summer flowers and glossy, green leathery foliage that will deal with Daylesford frosts! I'm happy!

Myrna Ellery, Daylesford, Vic

Espalier

Espalier — the age-old practice of pruning and training plants to grow on a flat surface — is a wonderful way to grow largish plants in a small garden. Camellias, fruit trees and ornamental trees can all be trained this way. As a general rule, to keep espalier looking good, carry out any heavy pruning in winter, train the new growth through spring and summer, and trim the secondary outward growths in autumn.

Nola McRae, Wagga Wagga, NSW

Magical May bush

If you're starting a new garden, why not grow a soft-leaved evergreen May bush? It is a hardy low-maintenance plant that's easy to trim. It's also very tolerant of dry conditions — mine has survived its eighth year of drought and still blooms stunningly every spring, when it attracts beautiful birds, butterflies and bees. As a hedge, the soft-textured green leaves are more appealing than any box hedge. My grandmother and mother introduced me to the joy of May bush walkways, something different and easy-care that should not be forgotten.

Margaret Grossman Pullen, Wangaratta North, Vic

Grow them on

My garden is always well covered in pea straw mulch. It's the secret to my healthy soil, but when I plant small seedlings of flowering annuals, they often get smothered in the mulch and rot. To overcome this, I plant my seedlings into little polystyrene cups that have drainage holes punched in the base. Once they grow to a good size, they're ready to survive being planted out. They also make terrific little gifts.

Meredith McQueen, Sandy Bay, Tas

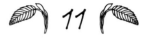

Australian natives

More and more gardeners are discovering the benefits of growing Australian native plants. In design, no other group of plants fits in with our landscape quite like our very own native flora, and the variety of foliage and flowers is both unique and endless. They make important habitats for our fauna, and in a time when water is at a premium, growing hardy local plants just makes good gardening sense.

There's still so much more to learn about using native plants, which is a very exciting prospect indeed. Some of our most passionate enthusiasts from across the country have shared enough of their experiences to whet our appetites.

Caterpillar control

Melaleucas will often get attacked by a webbing caterpillar. You'll see the dense webbing on the tips of the leaves and maybe some dead leaves and grub excreta. I find the best thing to do is trim them off. It breaks the cycle of the pest and keeps the numbers down.
Tony Wootton, Maleny, Qld

Perfect drainage

Don't plant grevilleas or banksias in heavy soil. I have learnt the hard way, having lost many of these plants to root rot.

Alison Edmonds, Corinda, Qld

Against all odds

I didn't think it possible, but I am growing beautiful Geraldton wax in my Central Queensland garden, where they usually fall to a dismal death. How did I do it? I tried to mimic its natural conditions by planting it in its own raised mound of introduced — and quite sandy — soil. I added some lime as well to raise the pH. Geraldton wax like a pH of between 7 and 9.

Gerald Drysdale, Rockhampton, Qld

Lessons learnt

The biggest gardening lesson I have learnt is to value and plant Australian native plants, especially those that are indigenous to my area. This ensures our bushland remains pristine and weed-free. It also means our garden fits in with the environment and plants are relatively trouble-free because they have been 'selected' to grow here. The result is a colourful display of unique and varied plants — plus visiting birds that fill the air with their music.

Jan Robilliard, Kalaru, NSW

Beautiful bark

Eucalypt trunks look marvellous in the larger garden. Their bark comes in a range of colours and textures. Some gums have smooth bark, while ironbarks, peppermints and stringybarks have attractive rough-textured bark. A mix of eucalypts in a grove, with different types of bark, is an eye-catching landscape feature.

Warren Sheather, Yarrowyck, NSW

Better backyard gum trees

Nothing says Australia like a gum tree, but some gardeners make the mistake of planting large eucalypts in suburban gardens. Big gum trees will undoubtedly cause expensive problems. They drop limbs at will, fill gutters with leaves and undermine foundations of buildings and pathways. But not all eucalypts develop into giants. Species like the red flowering gum from the south of Western Australia and the swamp bloodwood from northern Australia can be grown as tall shrubs or small trees. We call these species backyard eucalypts because they are safe to grow in most suburban gardens. Many backyard eucalypts have the most attractive flowers and will often bloom after only 3 years in the ground.

Warren Sheather, Yarrowyck, NSW

Hardy native hedges

Looking for a hardy, fast-growing hedge that will flower for most of the year? Then think about planting the native shrub, westringia. *Westringia fruticosa*, *W. longifolia* and *W.* 'Wynyabbie Gem' are ideal varieties that may be grown as low-to-medium-sized hedges. Their fine foliage clips beautifully for a formal look or you can prune them lightly with secateurs from time to time for a more informal hedge.

Warren Sheather, Yarrowyck, NSW

Show them the secateurs

Wattles (acacias) have a reputation for being short-lived plants that are prone to borer attack. Regular pruning will extend their lives considerably and reduce the risk of borer attack. After flowering, prune the branch just behind the spent blooms. This promotes a tremendous flush of healthy new growth and encourages a bounty of blooms in the following season. Start pruning your wattle after the very first time it flowers, then follow up with a good chop every year and your wattle tree will remain healthy and give you many years of pleasure.

Warren Sheather, Yarrowyck, NSW

Native clematis

Native clematis is a vine that makes an attractive cover to soften supports of patios and verandas. Every spring, the vines are loaded with white flowers. The interlocking branches and dense foliage provide safe nesting sites for small native birds.

Warren Sheather, Yarrowyck, NSW

Wild food source

When you're pruning your native trees and shrubs, don't waste all of those lovely young shoots and tips. Contact your local wildlife shelter and see if any of the trimmings are suitable for the animals they are caring for.

Lisa McClean, Hillcrest, NSW

Lawns

Love it or loathe it, the great Aussie lawn is here to stay. It's hard to imagine a weekend in the suburbs without that familiar chorus of lawnmowers. Many advocate that paved and pebbled surfaces are better than turf because they're both labour- and water-saving, but there's still a big group of nostalgic lawn lovers who believe there's nothing quite like the feeling of grass beneath your bare feet. I guess it's hard to find a more economical, versatile and hardwearing surface than turf.

One good thing, the ratio of lawn to garden bed is getting smaller — that means less mowing. Gardeners are also opting for drought-hardy species and they're being rewarded with lawns that are greener for longer. But most importantly, we are all learning not to waste valuable drinking water on the grass.

Laying down the lawn

Walking over newly laid turf will make the surface lumpy and uneven. A good way to avoid this is to lay boards or planks of timber over the freshly laid areas. It helps to pack the turf down at the same time.

Bob Davis, Stratford, Qld

Level-headed plan

Level lawn areas catch and hold moisture for much longer than sloping areas. If you want to have green grass without using much water, create level areas or terraces for lawn. You will find they're more functional and easy to use as well.

Cal Fishpool, Mt Cotton, Qld

Top turf choice

When I was looking for a drought-hardy turf for my place, buffalo was recommended. I have found it to be a hardwearing grass that seems to stay pretty green, even through the dry times.

Wayne Tritton, Sydenham, NSW

Thirst quencher

Using Velcro straps, attach a drinking bottle filled with cold water to the handles of your lawn mower. It's an easy way to keep cool and hydrated on a hot day.

Ross Dowel, Korumburra, Vic

Mow and feed in one

Over 20 years ago, I made one of the best purchases ever for both my lawn and myself. It's a mulching mower that chops the clippings very finely and returns them to the lawn. There's no heavy catcher to push and drag about, and the lawn and soil are fed as you mow. At first, my neighbours were scratching their heads wondering where the clippings were going. Now one of them has bought one himself.

Noeleen Ridgway, Ringwood North, Vic

Better water penetration

I like to keep a big bag of granular wetting agent in the shed. Once a year in spring, if there looks like some rain about, I get out and sprinkle it on my lawn. It seems to make a difference as even a small shower of rain is absorbed, giving the lawn a quick green lift.

Maureen Henderson, Golden Grove, SA

Makes good sense

Instead of washing my car on the road or driveway, I do it on the lawn. There's no water being wasted down the drain, and the lawn gets a good drink.

Denise Kerr, Alstonville, NSW

Clean 'em out

If you get patches of brown in your lawn and you can't quite fathom what it is, mix up a warm sudsy brew with washing powder — or, better still, catch it from your washing machine — and pour the solution all over the patches. If it's lawn grub, they will soon rise to the top.

Eve Nathan, Darlinghurst, NSW

Future looks sweeter

If you think you have lawn grubs, try treating the affected areas with a solution of molasses. Dissolve ? cup molasses in a bucket of water and saturate the soil with the solution. It dehydrates them.

Jenny Kershaw, Lismore, NSW

Controlling nutgrass in a lawn

There are selective herbicides for controlling nutgrass weed in lawns but they tend to be expensive, especially if you only have a small patch. I have found an alternative approach which is both economical and effective. Start by mowing your lawn. Do this at a time of year when the nutgrass [QUERY] is growing vigorously. The weed will grow back much quicker than your lawn and will soon be standing up well clear of the cut grass. Next take a heavy-duty PVC glove and super-glue a small patch of sponge onto the tips of the index finger and thumb. Then dip them into the recommended solution of glyphosate and run them up the leaf blades. It takes a little time but it will kill the nutgrass without killing your lawn. Follow up the process in a few weeks to get the ones you've missed.

Peter Chapman, Scarborough, Qld

Tea-riffic idea

If you need to patch up a small bare spot in your lawn, put down a used teabag then sprinkle grass seed on top of it. The tea bag acts like a little moisture reservoir to help get the seed off to a good start.

Julie Buxton, East Victoria Park, WA

Greener winter lawn

Many lawns can look drab and colourless over the winter months. I find that when I feed my lawn with a fertiliser high in potash, it tends to make it far more resistant to cold weather, keeping it looking healthier and greener for longer.

Robyn Noel, Wynvale, SA

Container gardening

You don't need to have a big backyard to experience the joy of growing something. That's where the marvellous flexibility of container gardening comes in. It allows us to grow plants wherever we choose while giving us the added benefit of being able to control the growing conditions to achieve optimum plant health. Dedicated gardeners from every corner of the country are growing all sorts of plants on balconies and patios, on courtyards and indoors, and they are getting the most brilliant results.

Here, some of them share their most valuable ideas and experiences.

Runaway restrained

To stop your potting mix escaping from the bottom of your pots, line the base of your container with a single piece of newspaper. It also helps to retain a little extra moisture in the mix.

Ray Reese, Pacific Pines, Qld

Tip for tea totallers

Save your used tea bags after that cup of tea. These little bags make excellent covers for the drainage holes in your pots.

1. They stop potting mix escaping the drainage holes.
2. They act like a little moisture reservoir for the plant.
3. They inhibit the entry of earwigs, slaters and ants.

Elizabeth Tozer, Paynesville, Vic

Pot-cleaning solution

Before reusing your old plastic pots, give them a good clean-up by soaking them in a solution of 1 part vinegar to 2 parts water.

Thelma Dennis, Bundanoon, NSW

Big pot vs small pot

I find that large pots tend to hold moisture longer than small pots. They don't heat up as much, either. I grow all my little things together in big pots and get far better results than I do when I try to grow them in their own individual small pots.

Beryl Morrison, Bongaree, Qld

Lighten the load

When you're growing displays of shallow-rooted plants like annuals in large deep pots, the bottom half of the mix is almost wasted. I like to fill the bases with foam balls or broken-up pieces from polystyrene boxes. It makes the pots much lighter and easier to move around and you save a lot of money on potting mix.

Del Patterson, Bulimba, Qld

Magical maidenhair

Here's my secret for growing magnificent maidenhair ferns in pots. Use a good-quality potting mix, plant up your fern, and spread the top with blood and bone. Keep the plant moist at all times — they love humidity — and find a sheltered position out of the drying wind. In July, cut the fern right back to its base, scrape about 2cm of potting mix off the top, replace it with some fresh potting mix and, once again, sprinkle the top with blood and bone. It's a no-fail way to achieve abundant healthy maidenhair.

Betty Dent, Wentworth Falls, NSW

Meat another winner

Terracotta pots look attractive but they can dry out very quickly. Here's a simple solution! Line the insides with little polystyrene meat trays. They make good insulators as well. Sheets of used aluminium foil also work well.

Barbara Wickes, Buderim, Qld

Swell suggestion

We find the best way to water our hanging baskets is to soak them in a bath. Then we sit them on a bucket to drain. That way the water can be saved and reused. Sometimes, rehanging the heavy wet baskets can be a physically demanding task. To overcome this we have installed a simple pulley and rope system to raise and lower baskets.

Chris Hughes, Geraldton, WA

No more hang-ups

Lowering heavy hanging baskets to the ground can be tricky, especially when the hooks are up high. I've come up with a method that makes it easy. Get hold of a long length of aluminium rod. Saw a slit in one end and push it apart slightly to form a 'V'. When you are lowering your baskets, take the weight of the pot in one hand and with the other, take the rod and use the 'V' end to lift the ring off its hook. An old broom handle could work just as well.

Joan Hanley, Emu Plains, NSW

Cool idea

Here's a way to water your hanging baskets without lifting heavy watering cans or spilling and wasting water from a hose. Every day, give them a couple of ice cubes. The ice melts slowly, wetting the potting mix without leaving a big puddle on the floor.

Spence & Lyn Grubb, Deception Bay, Qld

It's in the bag

I have always had trouble with my hanging baskets drying out too quickly, particularly the types that have the coconut fibre liners. These days, I put a plastic shopping bag inside the liner to reduce the moisture loss. I cut off the handles and make some holes for drainage before adding the potting mix. It works beautifully and saves my water and plants.

Margaret Auld, Merredin, WA

Worms in pots

Worms are great for the soil, but not so good to have in your pot plants. A simple way to rid your pots of earthworms is with a pale pink mixture of Condy's crystals (potassium permanganate). Water it in, and the worms quickly evacuate.

Noeleen Ridgway, Ringwood North, Vic

Ants in your plants

If you have trouble with ants getting into your pot plants, try sprinkling a little derris dust on top of the mix and around the base of your pots.

Thea Wall, Lismore, NSW

It won't let you down

If I'm going away for a few days, I spray the foliage of my pot plants with an antitranspirant. I find it helps to keep the plants alive when the potting mix dries out.

Alison Lee, Belmont Heights, Qld

Better bonsai

Many people have trouble keeping their bonsai looking good, but if you bear in mind these tips, your bonsai will thrive.

1. Keep it moist.

2. Give it plenty of fresh air.

3. Give it good sunlight.

4. Feed it regularly in small amounts during the growing season.

5. Trim it regularly to maintain its shape.

6. Re-pot it every 2 to 3 years.

7. Don't keep it indoors — display it inside for short periods only.
Leigh Taafe, Charnwood, NSW

Pot feet

I have found that sitting terracotta pots on a set of pot feet helps promote better drainage, which brings out the best in your blooms.
Nola McRae, Wagga Wagga, NSW

Rubber protectors

When I used saucers under my pot plants, the plants would often suffer from 'wet feet'. I have since removed all the saucers and now stand the pots on reused rubber doormats cut to size. They protect the surface beneath while allowing the pots to drain freely.

Annie Little, Gosnells, WA

14

Vegetables

More and more Australian gardeners are getting into growing their own organic veggies. In many cases, it's because people are concerned about where their food is coming from, how fresh it is and what sort of chemicals have been sprayed on it. They are also concerned about the effects that these poisons are having on their health and the state of the precious soil they are being grown on. For others, they know that nothing tastes better than veggies that have just been harvested from the backyard, and they're jam-packed with vitamins and minerals. There's simply nothing more satisfying.

Here are some fresh ideas from Aussie gardeners who are totally addicted to their darling veggie patch.

TOMATOES

Fine-tuning tip

This tip is a development of a very good idea I found in the first *Garden Guru* book (ABC Books). It suggested using an upright cylinder of ordinary chicken wire as a method for supporting tomato plants. I tried this, with excellent results, and have since found a way to refine the idea. I arranged a series of tomato stakes in a zigzag pattern down the centre of a long bed and weaved a length of wire mesh through them. Then I planted a tomato plant in each V of alternate sides. It supported the plants very well without much additional effort, and the plants were more accessible.

John Stubbs, Rosebank, NSW

Befriend a plumber

This tip is probably most useful for tomato-growing plumbers or people who know plumbers who don't grow tomatoes. One day a plumber came to replace the sacrificial anode in our hot water system. It's a long rod made of a combination of metals that corrode readily, which helps protect and prevent corrosion of the metal hot water tank. The plumber said that his father uses them as stakes for tomatoes. I cut one in half and tried it for myself and I really think they help the plants to become more vigorous plants.

John Stubbs, Rosebank, NSW

Bags of tomatoes

If you're having trouble growing tomatoes in your soil, why don't you try growing them in hessian bags? I half-fill bags with a good-quality potting mix and old cow poo and put them in a sunny spot among other plants. 'Sweet bite' grows beautifully like this, and the plants look great in the garden. When the bag rots down, the whole lot can be spread over the garden.

Jan Gray, Willetton, WA

Stake-free

Try my method for supporting tomato plants without staking and constant tying. Take 2 or 3 sheets of weldmesh (2000mm by 700mm) and wire them on in layers or tiers to 6 metal stakes — one in each corner and one on each side at the centre. Place this frame structure in your garden and plant your seedlings beneath the first layer of mesh. The central leaders of the plants grow up through the mesh layers while the fruit-laden side shoots grow outwards, all supported off the ground without any tying or staking.

Roberta McLean, Violet Town, Vic

Dusty grubs

Somebody told me that to keep grubs out of your tomatoes, you should dust the blooms with flour as soon as they appear. It has worked for me, but you must remember to reapply it after rain.

G Grew, Ballina, NSW

Native plants and tomatoes

We don't have formal vegetable garden beds but every spring we plant tomatoes in new gardens with our native plants. Roma and Tommy toes are our varieties of choice. They produce large crops. Some tomatoes are not harvested and fall to the ground. In the following season the tomato seeds germinate at random. We harvest quantities of fruit from these feral tomatoes.

Warren Sheather, Yarrowyck, NSW

POTATOES

Super spud cylinder

I grow my seed potatoes in a plastic soak-well placed on the ground in my garden bed. The slits in the side allow for airflow and good drainage, and as the plants grow, I top up the cylinder with soil and compost. When the leaves have reached the top and died back, I simply lift off the lightweight container and watch the spuds fall at my feet. It's cheap and easy to do, and there's no grubbing around searching for potatoes.

KL Winn, Bunbury, WA

Intense cropping

For many years, I have planted and harvested 3 crops of potatoes a year from the same bed. This is how I go about it. When planting, I incorporate plenty of compost, a few handfuls of crushed rock minerals, a sprinkle of dark brown sugar and some potash. Then I plant the potatoes as normal, lay a soaker hose to water the plants, and cover with about 60cm of pea straw. I keep the whole thing moist and harvest my lovely spuds in just 12–14 weeks, always saving some egg-sized potatoes for the crop after next.

Robert Healy, Grovedale, Vic

Ruby red rhubarb

I have fond childhood memories from the 1960s of visiting my grandfather's veggie patch in Ballarat North. He grew a variety of marvellous vegetables, but the most memorable of all was his rhubarb. It was tall and thick and a very dark ruby red colour. This was his 'secret tip'. After boiling up some home-grown beetroot, he would toss the peelings back into the cooking water then put it aside for a few hours to cool. He would pour the entire contents of the pot onto the rhubarb crowns. This, he believed, was what made his rhubarb so robust and full of colour. Each autumn in the Black Hill Hall (Ballarat North), they had a produce competition where Jim Ross's rhubarb was second to none. Now his 'secret' is out!

Janet Duffy, Bairnsdale, Vic

100% carrot germination

Carrot seed is especially fine and can be difficult to keep continually moist to ensure a good germination rate. Try what I do. After broadcasting carrot seed or sowing them in rows, cover them with approximately 2cm of fresh grass clippings. Press it all down with a flat board (a wooden concreter's float is ideal) to ensure the seed has good contact with the soil. Water this regularly, using a soft spray from the hose, to keep it moist. The grass clippings help to hold the moisture, which is so important for germination, while also helping to prevent weeds. You'll soon see the seedlings pushing their way through.

Jan Harding, Theresa Creek, NSW

Perpetual carrot harvesting

I learnt this method for growing carrots from a friend in Adelaide and have used it successfully for many seasons. Cultivate a raised bed — about 1m² — of not-too-heavily fertilised soil until it's friable. Then sprinkle two packets of carrot seeds over the whole area, preferably using two different varieties and with one producing larger carrots than the other. Start thinning and harvesting from a tiny baby carrot size. Eventually you finish with large ones, suitable for baking in foil and honey with a roast leg of lamb. Lovely!

John Stubbs, Rosebank, NSW

Summertime veggie success

The veggie patch can really suffer on a hot day. When the mercury is high, get out and cover your veg with a piece of shade cloth. A few empty plastic pots spotted throughout the patch will help keep the cloth up off the veg. It works well in the winter too and protects frost sensitive seedlings.

Richard Cox, Blacksnake, Qld

Great white radish

Giant white Japanese radishes are easy to cultivate. They grow long and thick and do a great job of opening up a hard and poorly drained soil.

Don MacKay, Margaret River, WA

Dangerous daikon

Here's a fun and interesting way to grow those long white Japanese radishes. Cut up sections of plastic plumbing pipe — at least 75cm long. Then sit them vertically on top of the soil and fill with good-quality potting mix and a sprinkle of phosphorus-rich fertiliser. Sow the radish seeds in the top, thin the excess seedlings after germination and make sure they don't dry out. The roots will develop beautifully down the length of the pipe, and harvesting is easy — no digging! Your long-rooted radishes will be superb when grated in salads or chopped into stir-fries.

Judy Horton, Dural, NSW

Worm seeds

I often germinate my vegetable seeds in the top of an open worm farm. The seeds come up in days and they develop rapidly in the rich moist castings — ready to plant into the veggie patch within 2 or 3 weeks.

John O'Reilly, Banora Point, NSW

Moon planting testimonial

I plant and sow by the moon. NEVER on a full moon or a new moon. That's the time for 'cleaning up'. After the 'new' moon, plant veggies that produce their crop above the ground. After the 'full' moon, plant veggies that produce their crop below the ground. An Italian neighbour in Canberra introduced me to this theory in 1974. He heard me 'cussing' about the fact that my newly planted spinach and lettuce had gone to seed. He was a great vegetable grower, as was his father back in Italy. From that day on, I have followed this rule and since then I have NEVER had a vegetable prematurely go to seed. I have sometimes had 5 crops from a bean planting. I have also been laughed at, but that's OK. My veggies don't go to seed!

Sandra Sigrid Capper, Mudgee, NSW

Companion planting

I have had tremendous success using capsicum as a companion plant with my roses. The shape and height of the capsicum bush is perfectly suited to fill the gap between the rose bushes. Both of them have benefited from the extra love and attention and have been highly productive together.

Dan Quigley, Macleod, Vic

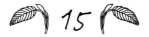

Herbs

Herbs are a totally fascinating and extremely valuable group of plants. There are herbs that repel pests and predators, others that attract beneficial insects to the garden. We have herbs that can be taken medicinally to cure illnesses and some that invigorate the mind and spirit or help us to be calm and relaxed. Perhaps the best known herbs are the wonderful ones we grow and harvest to flavour our favourite cuisine.

It doesn't matter how small the garden, people will always find a spot to care for a few of their beloved herbs. And their foliage, colours and textures always make a breathtaking display spilling out of an interesting pot.

Mozzie repellent

Do you get eaten by mozzies in the evenings? Soothe bites with freshly picked rosemary or lavender. Rub leaves or flowers over exposed skin, and the itch will soon disappear. You can also rub them over your arms and legs as a preventative.

Beverley Morgan, Shepparton, Vic

Mini mint garden

When it comes to growing mint, there's an old saying, 'Put the thing in a good strong pot or a garden you'll have not!' Make yourself a mini mint garden in a big pot with three types of mint — applemint, spearmint and peppermint. Start by lining the base of the pot with shade cloth. It will stop the mint from escaping through the drainage holes. When you've potted the mint plants, place the container in a partially shaded position and keep it well watered and well fed. You'll have plenty of fresh foliage for flavouring dishes and making refreshing cups of mint tea.

Patricia Ravaillion, Ulverstone, Tas

Mint invasion

If you like mint, try growing it in hanging water-well pots. It won't have a chance to invade your garden beds, and the plants will receive exactly the right amount of water to make it flourish. You can even put a diluted liquid fertiliser in the well to feed it.

Noeleen Ridgway, Ringwood North, Vic

Lemon sprinkles

If your chives start to wither, don't cut them down to soil level. Let them die off naturally and then sprinkle some lemon juice on them. They will grow back quicker and healthier than before.

Tracey Pocock, Grovedale, Vic

Italian parsley

After years of trying to grow good parsley, I am delighted by the results I get with Italian parsley. It's a hardy grower and produces masses of seeds. I just get the seed heads in my hand and throw them around the border of my garden. Next spring (or whenever they feel like it, really) they'll sprout again without any particular attention. Now I never seem to be without parsley.

Keiran Deasey, Prahran, Vic

More mint

I found that the snails in my garden would eat my common mint. But I put in some Vietnamese mint and they didn't touch it. My tip is on the propagation of Vietnamese mint. Pick bunches of it when it's growing well, in February/March, then bring it inside and place it in a glass of water in a light-filled area. In less than 2 weeks, it shoots new roots and is ready for planting out. Once you buy this mint you never have to buy it again as it is so easy to propagate. You can propagate it and sell it at the school fete!

Mrs Mai Margetts, Essendon, Vic

Kitchen herbs on hand

I use a lot of herbs for cooking and I like to have a selection of pots growing on the windowsill close at hand. But they don't get enough sun there so they don't thrive. Finally the solution dawned on me. Now I have two pots of everything — one lot out in my sunny courtyard and the other on the windowsill — and I rotate them regularly.

Alison Lee, Belmont, Qld

Herbs in the tropics

Tropical downpours can be extremely damaging to herbs up our way. I grow mine in pots so that I can move them out of the rain. If I'm planting in the ground, I incorporate a lot of sand and gravel in the planting hole so that excess moisture doesn't accumulate around the roots.

Lina Pasetti, Brinsmeed, Qld

16

Fruit

Sweet, delicious home-grown fruit, fresh from your backyard, in season and reaching its peak of ripeness as nature intended. There's really nothing better, and it's by far the best way to guarantee a harvest that's full of vitamins and free from harmful chemicals and pesticides.

From acreage gardens right through to tiny inner-city courtyards, inspiring gardeners are growing their own organic fruit with enormous success and huge returns. Along the way, their dedication and hard work have gained them considerable know-how and, thankfully, many of them have been willing to share it.

It's a boy! It's a girl!

Years ago when I lived in Darwin, a local indigenous woman taught me this trick for determining the sex of young paw paw trees. Raise your plants in pots first. Before planting them out, take a good look at the root system. If it's short and bunchy, then the plant is a female. In the case of males, you'll find that the roots are long and thin. I have grown many paw paw plants over the years, and this rule of thumb has rarely failed me.

Pamela Mathey, Alstonville, NSW

Twisting your melon

Typically, when a developing melon sits in one spot for an extended period, the side in contact with the ground can rot, destroying your melon. A simple way to avoid this is to give each developing fruit a little turn every few days. The bottom surface never has the chance to rot because it's not in contact with the ground for long enough. Also, all sides of the fruit get regular exposure to the sunshine, which helps to harden up the skin.

Luke Wall, Lismore, NSW

Twice the value

If you need a hedge in your garden, why don't you plant a row of fruit trees like citrus or stone fruit or, for a smaller hedge, try raspberries, loganberries or blueberries. You end up with a screen or boundary for your garden plus bucketfuls of fruit to enjoy.

Barry Cline, Stanhope, Vic

Avocado anytime

Have you got too many ripe avocadoes? Then why don't you freeze them? Scoop all the pulp into a bowl, mash it and mix it with lemon juice. Then put the seed back in, place the mix into an airtight plastic bag or container and freeze. Now you have avocado on call, ready for whipping up a quick guacamole. It works beautifully, but you've got to put that seed in!

John Mayall, Uralba, NSW

New lease of life for lemons

My lemon tree was producing beautiful fruit for many years, until one season the lemons started to go dry and woody. An older gardener friend told me it was because my soil was deficient in trace elements. I took his advice, purchased some trace element mix and applied it to the soil. It worked, and now my lemons are sweet and juicy again.

Brett Gordon, Redcliffe, Qld

Caution — collar rot

Citrus trees are tough as a rule, but if the bark at the base is damaged, a disease called collar rot can enter and kill them by ringbarking the tree. Usually you don't see the signs of collar rot until it's too late. A good indication is when the tree puts on a big flush of flowers but has hardly any foliage to support it. There's little you can do to save it when it gets to this stage. Be careful not to damage your trees with your brush cutter, wheelbarrow or spades. Check your trees regularly. If you see any signs of damaged or rotting bark at the base of the trunk, try treating it in the following way. Scrape any mulch away from the base of the tree — it can cause and speed up the rotting process. Expose the affected area. Mix up a bucket of bleach according to directions and use it to scrub the base of the tree. Bleach is a powerful fungicide. Remove and discard any dead bark and apply more bleach solution to the wound. If the tree is not completely ringbarked and there is still some live bark linking the roots to the crown, the tree may survive. If the tree is totally ringbarked, it's time to think about planting another one.

Michael Yonwin, Thorneside, Qld

Working miracles

Living in Sydney, I never thought I'd be able to grow tropical pineapples. Still, I had a go at growing one in a big black plastic pot in a warm spot. The plant grew beautifully and made an interesting pot plant. Lo and behold, almost 2 years later, we harvested the fruit. It was delicious and well worth the wait.

Vicki Cashin, Bronte, NSW

Suc`seeded`

50 years ago, I set out to grow an orchard from seed and I have succeeded. Now I have a wonderful range of fruiting trees — macadamias, citrus, mangoes, apples, and plums — all planted from seed. You do have to wait a little longer for some of them to bear fruit, but it does happen. Don't let anyone tell you can't grow fruit trees from seed.

Michael Yonwin, Thorneside, Qld

Fruity frames

Many gardeners cover their fruit trees with netting to keep birds from attacking their crop. The problem is that the nets get caught on the foliage so they're tricky to put on and remove. To get around the problem, I have come up with a modular netting system that's easy to assemble and pull down as required. It's a series of netted rectangular frames up to 1800mm wide and 2800mm tall (depending on the height of the tree you wish to protect). The frames are made from lengths of 38mm by 19mm treated pine which are joined with screws and simple halving joints. A square frame (1800mm wide) is made for the top. To assemble, you stand the 4 side frames around the tree, tie them together with string then tie on the square top. Depending on the shape and size of the tree, you may need extra side panels, making the shape of the top either pentagonal or hexagonal. Once the frame is up, all you need to do is release the strings on one side when you want to access the tree. The frames are solid, so they keep troublesome possums out as well. You can also use the frames over bushes like berries. Simply tie 2 together like an A-frame and use some loose netting to cover the ends.

George Loughborough, Beaconsfield, Tas

Pipe protection

This is an easy frame for bird netting that can be knocked up in minutes. Drive 4 star pickets into the ground around your tree. Then cut 2 lengths of heavy black irrigation poly-pipe to form a diagonal arch frame over the tree. The ends of the pipe slip easily and firmly over the star pickets. Tie the pipe in the centre, where they cross, and slip your netting over this. It's just as easy to dismantle and set up elsewhere when needed.

John Hanlon, Gordon, Tas

Delicious strawberries

When we started growing our own strawberries, we discovered what a true strawberry tasted like. There was a hitch, however: we always had a spring–early summer crop but few fruit throughout the remainder of the year. That was until we discovered how to get more out of our plants. Every autumn, we plant fresh new runners that have formed on last year's plants. We carry out regular watering and feeding with our homemade worm compost tea and seaweed extract. Another discovery is that 1 or 2 applications of sulphate of potash seem to stimulate an extra crop in late summer, extending our harvest period of these magnificent sweet strawberries.

James Cherry, Nemingha, NSW

Heart of the problem

If your fruit vines are healthy but aren't bearing any fruit or flowers, then try this tip, given to me by my elderly mother. On the main stem, about 10cm above the ground make a vertical slit about 3cm long that pierces right through the stem. Then insert a stick in the hole. It will make your vine produce flowers and fruit. It sounds drastic, but I've tested it on my gourd vine and it worked brilliantly.

Nguyet Tran, Clayton, Vic

Try this in your trap

If you have a problem with fruit fly, get hold of some plastic bottles, tip a little diesel in them, and hang them about your trees. For some strange reason, the fruit flies are attracted to the diesel; they enter the plastic trap and die. Just make a hole in the bottle for easy entry.

Jan Heathwood, Caboolture, Qld

Fruit fly barrier

To keep fruit fly out, I made some bags to cover the fruit, using old fine netting curtain material. I threaded some nylon fishing line through the tops of the bags, which makes it easy to secure them quickly. They work extremely well, and you can use them over and over again.

Judy Wilson, Mullumbimby, NSW

Fruitful partnership

Quite by chance, I discovered that citrus and macadamia trees have a remarkable affinity. If each tree's foliage touches, both trees take off and grow vigorously. It's not enough to grow them in close proximity; they must actually touch to benefit. I had 6 nut trees planted out, of which 5 were coming into fruit. The sixth was thin and weedy with only a couple of long limp stems. About 2 metres from this grew a very old orange tree that was in decline. The wind blew the limp nut branch around and it hooked onto the orange branch. Both trees began shooting vigorously from all leaf joints. In 2 years, the nut had overtaken its siblings and produced the biggest and best nuts of all of them. The orange had a new lease of life and was covered in foliage, flowers and fruit. This was all without any attention from me. Both trees prospered for another 20 years until finally the old orange tree died. The nut literally went into mourning. It shed healthy branches for no apparent reason until it had lost two-thirds of its canopy.

Michael Yonwin, Thorneside, Qld

Give choko (another) go

Chokos are easy to grow but notoriously difficult to peel. An easy way to peel them is to rub oil on them first.

Pamela Mathey, Alstonville, NSW

Marvellous gardening innovations

Many of the world's best inventions have been nutted out somewhere in someone's back shed. The shed is more than simply a refuge from the pressures of everyday life. It's a magical place where new ideas are born and typical gardening problems are solved. Sure, some of the bizarre contraptions that emerge can look a little weird, but generally they work!

Here's a selection of some of the latest winners emerging from sheds across Australia.

This deserves a big hand

Cut 2 sides off a square 20-litre plastic drum. Then take each piece and make a couple of slots in them so that you can fix a leather strap to fit over your hands. These make sturdy 'garden hands' for picking up mulch, leaves, sweepings etc.

Jill Redwood, Goongerah, Vic

Deep-watering pipe

To help you water your plants deeply, get a length of PVC pipe that's 25mm in diameter and 2 metres long. Slip it over the end of the garden hose and plunge it into the soil around the root zone of your plants. This lets you water individual plants quickly and deeply, and it's a much more efficient use of water.

Lance Baister-Jones, Claremont, WA

Create a natural hanging planter

Don't waste those fallen palm fronds. You can use them to make hanging planters. Take a large fallen palm frond from a palm tree (Alexander palm fronds are good) and cut off the leafy section. It makes good mulch. Then take the hard end piece and soak it in water for 24 hours or so until it's soft enough to work with. Make a hole about 2cm away from the narrow cut end. Thread a wire hook through the hole for hanging purposes. Then grasp the hard piece at the bottom and bend it in half, flipping it up to the top. Fold in the sides and puncture holes through both sides, about 3 cm apart. Use some thick raffia to thread through the holes and join the pieces together to form a sack. In the cavity, you can place a potted plant or fill it with potting mix and plant directly into that. You now have a wonderful homemade gift for little or no expense.

Denise Lucas, Carindale, Qld

Mulch donut

The mulch around my trees was always being blown away by the wind or scratched up by birds, until now. I have created what I call the 'mulch donut'. Simply encase your mulch in bird netting, roll it up like a sausage and form a donut shape around the root zone of trees and shrubs. The 'mulch donut' is long lasting, and it keeps the mulch away from the sensitive stem of your plants as well.

Elaine Leditschke, Eudunda, SA

Blown away by brilliance

The wind can get so strong in my garden that it blows away the mulch from around my precious trees and shrubs. To keep it in place, I make a ring with a piece of fencing wire (with a hook and loop at alternate ends), place it over the mulch around the tree and hold it in place using some cheap tent pegs. It's very effective at keeping mulch in place, even in the windiest of conditions.

Alan Caldwell, Woodville, NSW

Stop wayward hoses

To stop your hose from being dragged across garden beds, irrigation spikes and other areas where you don't want it to go, plunge some thin wooden or metal stakes into the ground that will act as a kind barrier to the area. Then pop some old plastic drink bottles over the top of each stake, cutting the bottom off if necessary. As you move around, the smooth rounded shape of the bottles will help guide your hose where you want it to go.

Annie Little, Gosnells, WA

Gardener's tool bag

I've often admired the handy tool bag that carpenters use and it's inspired me to make my very own gardener's tool bag. It looks a lot like the carpenter's model and it's made from stretch denim material so it's strong and comfortable. On the front, I've put large pockets on either side to hold a trowel and a weeding tool. In the middle is a smaller pocket to house my secateurs. I've also attached a large butterfly clip to the front. That holds my gloves when I'm not using them. There's a strap with a buckle that goes comfortably around my waist. It's extremely handy — you never misplace those smaller tools — and I use it all the time in the garden.

Barbara Waters, Murwillumbah, NSW

The latest in gardening fashion

We gardeners in the tropics learn to be wily and create our own special look! Most of the time it's too hot to wear heavy long-sleeved shirts, but you still need protection from lacerations to the forearm when tending bromeliads and the like. Here's a solution. Cut the toes off your socks and slide them up over your forearm, toe-end first. The heels sit perfectly to give you elbow protection, and the ribbed tops of the socks make a snug wrist fit under your gloves. It's the latest gardening fashion accessory around my place. Mine are red!

Lolli Forden, Smithfield, Qld

Upstanding idea

I love my trusty old hand trowel for planting seedlings, but as I get older, it gets harder to kneel down for long periods. My son removed the old handle and replaced it with a long broom handle. Now I can prepare the small holes for planting from a standing position.
Doris Shultz, Bendigo, Vic

Stop corrosion

Some metal wheelbarrows corrode fairly rapidly. The best thing to do is to unbolt all the different parts, insert an insulating washer at all the joins — cut-up bits of ice-cream container will work — and then reassemble them. This stops the corrosive action caused by electrolysis between the different metals used for the legs, handles and body. However, what gardener has time for this stuff? A rusty wheelbarrow can always be filled with potting mix and planted up with flowers.
Sasha Stubbs, Rosebank, NSW

Handy stakes

Snip off healthy tall stalks of bracken fern and remove the head of foliage. You now have some tough, straight thin stakes that are easy to push into the soil. You'll find many uses for them and they last for years, even when wet.
Jill Redwood, Goongerah, Vic

Corker of an idea

When you use bamboo stakes in the ground or pot plants for supporting plants, they can cause nasty eye accidents if you're not careful. To prevent this, I use wine bottle corks to cover the pointy ends. It just means that every time I pick up a bundle of bamboo stakes, I have to buy another case of wine!

Thea Wall, Lismore, NSW

Peg pals

Spring-loaded pegs are excellent for training vines and climbers to fences. They're quick and easy to use, and you can unclip them when they're no longer needed and reuse them somewhere else.

Del Patterson, Bulimba, Qld

Out on a limb

When pruning, keep an eye out for lengths of limb that have a fork in them. They make a useful prop for holding up low branches and keeping heavily laden fruit trees from bending too far.

Jill Redwood, Goongerah, Vic

Shady alternative

A 2m square piece of shade cloth is very handy for moving prunings, weeds, mulch and grass clippings etc. It's much easier to drag these materials around than pushing them about in a wheelbarrow, especially when you are a DOL (dear old lady).

Barbara Price, Wardrop Valley, NSW

Keeping records

When I buy new plants, I copy the details from the label in an abbreviated form onto strips of white plastic cut from old yoghurt containers. With a hole punched in one end, you can attach the new label onto the plant with a strip of pantyhose. On the back of the original nursery label, I note when it was planted out and the approximate position in the garden then store it away for future reference.

Maureen Burton, North Tamborine, Qld

Bonza bin

I have an old plastic rubbish bin to which I've attached some sturdy rope handles with padding to protect my hands. There are some triangles cut out of the base so that it drains freely. I use it everywhere in the garden to collect weeds and prunings. It's big enough to hold quite a lot of clippings and light enough to carry or drag even when full. Perfect for a terraced garden or for those inaccessible little places no wheelbarrow can reach.

Elaine Harris, Burnie, Tas

Got it covered

I use small plastic novelty wire wastebaskets to cover seedlings and protect them from heat, wind and pests like birds, grubs, snails and slugs. They come in lots of colours and can be bought for around $2 in bargain shops everywhere.

Bruce Harriott, Cootamundra, NSW

Recycling and reusing

Reduce, reuse and recycle! It's such an important motto and it's no surprise that gardeners are among the best ambassadors for it. Many gardeners can't bear to throw away anything. Some would call this hoarding, but it's far cleverer than that. There are so many innovative ways that people are finding uses for what others would plainly call rubbish. All it takes is a little imagination to put waste to good use in your backyard.

Here are some ingenious discoveries we've 'recycled' from Aussie gardeners, just to get you started.

Keep that old couch

You can turn an old couch or chair into a fabulous and colourful seat for your garden. Remove the upholstery to expose the frame. Screw and glue cement sheets onto the flat surfaces, then cement over the cushions, using chicken wire to shape and reinforce the concrete. Paint your recycled handiwork with paving paint or get creative with tiles to make a mosaic — but be warned; mosaic art is highly addictive! You may find yourself covering every hard surface in your garden with broken tiles, old crockery, coloured pebbles, shells, and so on.

Jan Johnson, Emerald, Vic

Turning rubbish into art

Polystyrene pieces that are used to pack motor parts, computers and other appliances come in all sorts of unusual shapes. Don't throw them away; use them to add a bit of original 'folk art' to your garden. Glue a few together (choose an adhesive that won't eat into the polystyrene) and you can make some very interesting and 'arty' sculptures for your garden. Give them a coat of acrylic paint and they'll last for years.

Bruce Skeen, Doonside, NSW

Multitasking

You've probably seen someone somewhere using an old car wheel rim for a hose reel. It's a terrific way of reusing them, but there's another possibility. Find a piece of gutter guard or some similar sturdy netting material. Attach it to the bottom third of the rim. As well as a hose reel, you've now created a handy storage unit for sprinklers, small gardening utensils and gloves etc.

Kate Lloyd, Albany, WA

Free garden edging

Ready-mix concrete suppliers will often have huge numbers of test samples lying around. Generally, they are 100 mm in diameter and 300 mm long. They are ideal for making garden edging. You can lay them flat, end on end, or stand them up in a shallow trench. The best bit is they're FREE!

Geoff Tune, Millner, NT

Retro recycling

Remember those old round concrete borders so popular in the '70s for putting around shrubs and roses? They can make interesting gardens flowing with succulents and ground covers. Collect some up and stack them 4 or 5 high, then fill with potting mix.

Ross Dowel, Korumburra, Vic

Tanks for this recycling idea

Old corrugated-iron rain tanks cut to about 75cm high make a fabulous raised vegetable garden. Use it as your compost bin initially and then plant it up when it's half-full. The side helps to protect young plants from the wind. Also, bend a long length of poly-pipe over the top, burying or securing it at each end. It makes a good support for netting to keep the birds out or for shade cloth to protect tender plants on a hot day. It works brilliantly.

Carol Saul, Killabakh, NSW

Spray packs

I save all the spray packs from household products and reuse them for all my different sprays in the garden. Each one is labelled so I never get them mixed up and accidentally spray the bugs with herbicide or liquid-feed my weeds!

Cheryl Ingram, Noble Park, Vic

Holey hoses

What can you do with an old hose that's full of holes? You can use it as an irrigation pipe. It's stronger and more flexible than conventional irrigation piping, and you can pick them up cheaply at the tip or free on council pick-up piles. Simply drill holes where required with a 3mm drill bit and insert standard drippers and 15mm irrigation fittings like joiners, elbows and T pieces. Heat the hose in hot water to insert the fittings. When it cools, the fit is quite snug so you don't need clamps. Bend the ends of the hose and tie them with wire to stop the flow. If you want to pull out one of the drippers, use pebbles to fill the holes.

John McCuaig, Moffat Beach, Qld

Alligator clips

Don't waste those off-cuts of irrigation poly-pipe. You can turn them into 'alligator clips'. Simply cut them into 5cm lengths and slit them down the side. They are useful for fixing shade cloth to a frame, guiding plants onto to a stake or trellis and for any other use you can find.

Jill Redwood, Goongerah, Vic

Plastic plant protectors

A clear plastic soft drink bottle makes a handy little plant protector. Cut off the top and bottom and slit the side from the top to the bottom. Then open it up and press the long cut edges into the soil to form a half-cylindrical protective tunnel over your tender seedlings. It's excellent in winter on those colds nights.

Eve Nathan, Darlinghurst, NSW

Better use for baskets

Sick of the wire-type hanging baskets that always need watering? Remove the chain and the liner, turn it upside down and use it as a protector for young plants against those front-end loaders called blackbirds.

Sheila Bannister, Longford, Tas

Rags to riches

Why throw away your old rags when you can reuse them one more time in the garden? Fabric is soft, so when you cut rags up into strips, they make excellent ties for staking plants and tying climbers to fences and trellises. Just one rag gives you a wealth of ties, and you can use them again and again.

Annie Little, Gosnells, WA

Vine ties

Don't lose those little plastic bread bag ties. They are handy as a quick and easy way to secure vines and climbing vegetables to a wire or trellis.

John Harris, Carindale, Qld

Bright idea

If you have any old throwaway electrical cords, strip back the plastic coatings to reveal the colourful wires inside. They make excellent ties for plants that can be used again and again.

Kerrie Goodchild, Derby, WA

Flexible plant ties

Old fly-screen is quite soft and makes an excellent plant-tie. I like to cut it into strips and staple it to a stake to support my plants. It's strong yet flexible so it can expand a little as the plant grows.

Peter Sibly, Port Elliot, SA

Sturdy plant tags

Light-coloured Venetian blind slats make long-lasting plant tags. Cut them to any length you like and write on them with a permanent marker. Look out for them on council roadside collections.

Noeleen Ridgway, Ringwood North, Vic

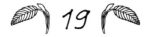 19

Reflections of a gardener

Working hard in the garden and watching things grow is the stuff that gives many people a deep sense of satisfaction and well-being. Sometimes it even inspires the poet within!

The joy that some individuals receive is expressed and shared in this fine collection of poetry and stories. And what a poetic bunch they are, too!

Heart, body and soul

Gardens are totally therapeutic. They love anything you do for them, they never argue, they make you feel good from the physical work, their colour, their beauty and their ever-changing moods. Who could ever live without a garden? All our family love what we have created as they have planted it, played in it, spread petals like confetti, photographed it and shared it with their friends. Gardening is my relaxation and love. I garden with my heart and body, which I am sure many others do.

Patricia Gabb, Beaufort, Vic

A very special place

My garden caters for all times of life
Times of happiness and times of strife
When I'm sad, it hides the tears,
That gives my grief release.
When I'm blue, it wraps me round
With such a sense of peace.
When I mourn it demonstrates
That life will still go on.
In happiness, its sights and scents
Both fill my heart with song.
When I'm feeling angry
And activity is needed,
There's always some corner
That's waiting to be weeded.
If I get downhearted,
Thinking life's not fair,
I know the special comfort
of my garden is still there.
In all the times of happiness and strife,
my garden is important in my life.

Helen Brumby, Rose Bay, Tas

I love my garden

Three years ago I had an unexpected interruption to work. This freed up some time for me, so I began to garden. To begin, I would walk around my area and visit the local park, which had streams, trees and shrubs. I began to appreciate the beauty of gardens in my local area and put time into developing what I had.

Some things I learnt along the way:

1. That weeds will grow prolific when the soil and garden are at their best.
2. Weeds are inevitable.
3. I know when my humble garden starts showing signs of deterioration, is time for me to take a break.
4. Weeds grow next to plants that are similar to trick us into thinking they're the real plant. (I once had a bush that grew 5m by 5m and it took me 3 months to discover it was not my original passionfruit vine!)
5. Snails are hungry buggers.
6. Nurture and you will be rewarded.
7. Cats will dig and poop in the garden.
8. Asparagus fern is not a good plant for my garden or the environment.
9. Break tasks up into small manageable chunks, otherwise gardening becomes a chore rather than a pleasure.

Advantages of gardening:
1. My husband is proud to show off my garden to every visitor.
2. I can share my garden with friends and relatives.
3. It keeps me moving — a pleasurable form of exercise.
4. When the chips are down, I walk around and say how much I love it.
5. It relieves tension — there's nothing like weeding or chopping when you're stressed.
6. Meeting people with the same interest and having common ground.

Major pitfalls:
1. Garden shops and magazines — I had to go back to work to pay for my habit!

I love my kangaroo paw, my magnolia, my peach tree, the smell of my jonquils, the sound of my fountain, the smile of my Buddha, the taste of my coriander, the sound of my feet crunching the autumn leaves under my favourite shoes, looking forward to flowers, planting whatever I like and learning as it grows, the smell of my lavender as I brush past while pruning my diosma, the colour and smell of the sweet pea that has made it to spring and not been dug up by the dog — reminding me how sweet spring is!

Belinda McFarlane, Yagoona, NSW

You've got to love it

'I saw the deer frolicking in your veggie garden again this morning,' my neighbour, Anne, tells me regularly. At least the deer aren't goats, which is what I thought they were when I first saw their hoof prints among the beans. Deer love beans, and strangely don't eat much else. My sweetcorn, seedlings and strawberries are all safe.

The wombat doesn't eat anything — another surprise — but follows predetermined pathways across my beds. Anything blocking her path, she moves or bulldozes down, and then leaves poos at my veggie garden gate. She discovered that bulldozing gets her through the garden gate at the base of the netting — and the deer bound up the rockery that surrounds half the garden.

My new garden, though, is sweetly simple compared to my last one which was installed on a remote beach in the Northern Territory. The property, up until relatively recently, belonged to indigenous Australians. My block used to be their garden, really. It's full of bush tucker trees and dingoes, wild horses, wallabies — and birds that, on discovering tomatoes, behave like miniature pterodactyls.

Building a veggie garden involved creating soil on top of the termite-ridden red ochre ferricrete. So I copied the Anglo-Australian early settlers' solution of putting soil into tins, pots and tyres placed on sheets of corrugated iron to keep out the termites.

Termites ate out the base of a new mango tree so quickly it keeled over while the tree was healthy and alive. One minute it was standing, the next gone.

The veggie garden then needed to be fenced, and after the tomatoes ripened and the pterodactyls appeared, it had to be covered with bird netting from fence to fence. Then the bird netting filled with mountains of leaves!

Veggie gardens have to be one of my favourite magical places, but I must admit, I keep out of my veggie gardens at the hottest times of the day in summer since the first and last time I went into the garden with my family to pick zucchinis. We had to wait for a tiger snake to leave. It's a bit unnerving eating zucchinis after watching a snake slither slowly over them.

Janis Embury, Warburton, Vic

Be patient

Don't expect too much from your garden, and then, when the plants are flowering, jump for joy. Have a little chat with a plant. It won't hurt. At the end of any day, get your cup of tea or coffee, wine or beer and walk around and enjoy your garden.

Cathy Stockton, Yenda, NSW

Bumble

Bumble on, sweet little bee,
Making honey in my tree.
Bumble, bumble round my garden
While you're thinking, 'Beg my pardon!'
They say, aeronautically,
There's no way that you can be
Flying, flying all around
And you should bumble on the ground.
They are wrong, for I can see
That you are air-borne perfectly,
Bumbling, bumbling by the hour,
Between the hive and pollened flower.
In your yellow/brown striped vest,
You are just the very best
At making honey! Little bee,
You *are* welcome in my tree.

Helen Brumby, Rose Bay, Tas

❀

Have you got a great gardening idea that you would like to share with the rest of us? It could be immortalised in a future Garden Guru book!

Send us your tips online at www.abc.net.au/backyard/gardening
or post them to the Garden Guru, ABC North Coast,
PO Box 908, Lismore 2480

Now, get back into yer garden — and I'll see you next time!

Phil Dudman, The Garden Guru